THE AUTOBIOGRAPHY OF
BENJAMIN FRANKLIN

• THE BARNES & NOBLE LIBRARY OF ESSENTIAL READING •

THE AUTOBIOGRAPHY OF BENJAMIN FRANKLIN

Benjamin Franklin

Introduction by Andrew S. Trees

BARNES & NOBLE BOOKS

NEW YORK

THE BARNES & NOBLE
LIBRARY OF ESSENTIAL READING

CONTENTS

INTRODUCTION

THE *Autobiography of Benjamin Franklin* is one of the most important and influential works in American history. It tells the story of Franklin's life from his humble beginnings to his emergence as a leading figure in the American colonies and, in the process, creates a portrait of Franklin as the quintessential American. Because of the book, he became a role model for future generations of Americans, who hoped to emulate his rags-to-riches story. The *Autobiography* has also become one of the central works not just for understanding Franklin but for understanding America.

Benjamin Franklin (1706-1790) was a man of many roles — printer, author, philosopher, scientist, inventor, diplomat, and politician, to name only a few. He lived a wide and varied life and found himself at the center of virtually every major event involving America during the second half of the eighteenth century. He was so successful as a businessman that he was able to retire at the age of 42. He proved equally adept at science, and his experiments in electricity made him the most famous American in the colonies. Politics and diplomacy occupied him for most of the latter half of his life, and he was a master of these as well. His *Autobiography* is essential reading for any attempt to come to terms with this complex and multifaceted man.

Born in Boston as the eighth child of ten to a pious Puritan family, Franklin knew from an early age that success would come only from his own efforts. After some initial indecision about his career, he was apprenticed to his brother James, who was a printer. The choice was a fortunate one. The profession would give Franklin an influence far beyond that of almost any other trade. Franklin chafed under what he considered his brother's overbearing manner, and he eventually broke his indentures and ran away in 1723 to Philadelphia, where he soon found a job with another printer. He opened his own printing shop a few years later. In 1729, he acquired a newspaper, the *Pennsylvania Gazette*. He also did most of the public printing in the colony and served as the postmaster for Philadelphia. In 1732, he began publishing *Poor Richard's Almanack,* which played an important role in establishing Franklin's wealth.

During his years in Philadelphia, Franklin played an increasingly influential role in the civic life of the city and the colony. He was actively involved in numerous voluntary ventures to improve life in Philadelphia, a practical application of many of the ideas that would find expression later in his *Autobiography*. In 1731, with a group of friends, he established the first circulating library in America, which came to be emulated throughout the colonies. He founded a fire company (1736), the American Philosophical Society (1743), a college that later became the University of Pennsylvania (1749), an insurance company (1751), and a city hospital (1751). He also organized a number of other improvements in city life, such as streetlights and street cleaning. In his *Autobiography*, Franklin wrote, "Human Felicity is produc'd not so much by great Pieces of good Fortune that seldom happen, as by little Advantages that occur every Day"—an apt summation of Franklin's pragmatic and commonsense approach to life.

After his retirement, Franklin busied himself with science and performed a variety of experiments with electricity. He eventually came up with a theory to explain electricity in its various forms, a breakthrough that led to his election to England's Royal Society (1756) and to the French Academy of Sciences (1772). His discoveries made him the most famous American in the thirteen colonies. As always, Franklin looked for practical applications of his theory and invented the lightning rod to protect buildings against lightning strikes. Lightning rods soon began to appear on buildings throughout the world.

Increasingly, though, Franklin's retirement was spent in public service. He was elected to the Pennsylvania Assembly in 1751 and spent virtually the rest of his life in one governmental post or another. In 1757, he was sent to London as the representative of the Pennsylvania Assembly to argue on behalf of the colony that the power of the colony's proprietors should be curbed. He returned to America in 1762, then went back to London two years later to try to convince officials to change Pennsylvania from a proprietary colony to a royal colony, although the growing conflict with England quickly changed Franklin's agenda. While he diligently worked to bring the two sides together, he argued forcefully for the rights and liberties of Americans and bluntly told British officials that the colonials would never accept an abridgment of those liberties. During this time, Franklin came to view himself as an American, rather than as a citizen of the British Empire. A number of other colonies eventually appointed him as their representative in London as well, and he became the leading spokesman for America in Great Britain during the crucial prerevolutionary years. After a severe upbraiding before the English Privy Council for leaking private letters that helped inflame colonial sentiment against the Massachusetts royal governor, Franklin left England in 1775. He was elected to the second Continental Congress, and in 1776 he found himself recrossing the Atlantic to try to persuade the French government to support the American Revolution. The literary and scientific community quickly embraced him as an embodiment of the natural virtues extolled by the *philosophes*, and he successfully negotiated an alliance between France and America that was essential to America's eventual victory. When the war ended, he helped negotiate the Treaty of Paris with Great Britain and returned to Philadelphia in 1785. He attended the Constitutional Convention, although he did not play a significant role in the debates, and he worked for the cause of abolition in the final years of his life.

Although Franklin's long and illustrious career ensured that he would hold a central place in early American history, his *Autobiography* played a crucial role in cementing his reputation as the prototypical American. The work has a complicated history of composition and publication, which is part of the reason why readers often find the work—and Franklin himself—elusive. It was written in four parts. Franklin wrote the first part in July and August of 1771, ostensibly addressing it as advice to his son, William, although that was likely only a literary device because William was already the governor of New Jersey. He also drew up a list of topics that he wanted to address in the work.

Franklin wrote the second part in France in 1784 and included two letters from admirers of the first part who urged him to continue the work. Franklin's inclusion of those letters gave a kind of justification to his work and revealed what a revolutionary undertaking it was. What made it revolutionary was what made Franklin himself revolutionary—his *Autobiography* was not the work of a king, or an aristocrat, or a general but the work of a man who had begun life as a poor tradesman. For a man such as that to write an autobiography was to do more than simply recount a life—it was to reveal a revolution in society. Birth and one's initial place in society's hierarchy were no longer the sole criteria for defining one's importance—at least in American society. Although early America was not completely free of social stratification, it was a remarkably fluid society and offered ample scope for Franklin and others to rise to prominence through merit alone.

In 1788, after retiring from the presidency of Pennsylvania, Franklin wrote the third part, which was also the longest. Sometime before his death in April 1790, Franklin added the fourth section, which was only seven and a half pages. Franklin also revised the different sections at various points.

The work's publication followed a circuitous path. Although various versions appeared in print, usually translated from French, the first authorized English version did not appear until 1818, and even this version did not include the fourth part. The complete work was not printed in English from the original manuscript until 1868. Despite all of this, the work quickly became a perennial best-seller in the nineteenth century as countless young boys turned to it as a guidebook for success, with Franklin as the perfect model of industry and virtue.

The extended period of the *Autobiography*'s composition left its imprint on the work. When Franklin originally wrote the first part, he still thought of himself as an Englishman and was proud to be one. By the time he began the second section, however, the American Revolution had changed his self-perception entirely, and in his writing he consciously recast himself as an American. The first part adheres largely to a chronological order and often reads like a picaresque novel with its young, somewhat naïve narrator learning to make his way in the world. The second part focuses mainly on Franklin's plan for moral perfection and is generally the section that has led to the most criticism. Many have seen it as proof of Franklin's impoverished spirituality and his materialism. But Franklin was far from the simple narrator that he seemed to be. A sly irony runs through the section, alerting readers to Franklin's own knowledge of the somewhat ridiculous nature of his quest. In the third and fourth sections, we see Franklin in the role of a leading citizen of Philadelphia, as well as frequent examples of the problems with English rule in the late colonial period. Throughout the work, Franklin remains a somewhat elusive figure — the very artlessness of the writing disguises not just a master prose stylist but a man who constantly and consciously shaped his image for public consumption.

Franklin's *Autobiography* gave definitive expression to many elements of what would come to be seen as the American character. He was a proselytizer for the power of individualism, showing in countless examples from his own life how one man could change society. He was also an eternal optimist. Perhaps most importantly, he came to embody the American dream, the idea that anyone, no matter how humble his or her background, could rise to the highest level in society.

For most of the nineteenth century, Franklin's book served as a primer for how to succeed. Even in the twentieth century, the *Autobiography* remained a central work, but a more critical appraisal of Franklin began to occur. Max Weber famously saw Franklin as the perfect embodiment of the spirit of capitalism, claiming that Franklin articulated "a philosophy of avarice... which is assumed as an end in itself.... Man is dominated by the making of money, by acquisition as the ultimate purpose of life." Other commentators often took a similarly harsh view. They argued that he was an artful hypocrite, disguising his true character behind a façade of facile pieties about frugality and hard work, even as he lived the life of a wealthy eighteenth-century gentleman, or they saw him as a symbol of how Americans had an impoverished view of life dominated by shallow materialism. D. H. Lawrence complained:

> Now if Mr. Andrew Carnegie, or any other millionaire, had wished to invent a God to suit his ends, he could not have done better. Benjamin did it for him in the eighteenth century. God is the supreme servant of men who want to get on, to *produce*.... But man has a soul, though you can't locate it either in his purse or his pocket-book or his heart or his stomach or his head. The *wholeness* of a man is in his soul. Not merely that nice comfortable bit which Benjamin marks out.

But many would say that those criticisms confuse the literary persona with the man, and Franklin's own life belies any easy reduction of him to a materialist. He spent most of his life in public service, not trying to increase his fortune. As for his hypocrisy, defenders claim that he was gifted at fashioning a self to suit his audience and that he used this ability not to deceive anyone but to further what he saw as the public good.

Regardless of one's view, Benjamin Franklin provided the definitive early template for success in a rapidly expanding country and an early formulation for what came to be called the American dream. America as a land of opportunity, as a place where anyone can rise to wealth and prominence through hard work rather than birth, found full expression in Franklin's writings. And the *Autobiography* remains a touchstone of American history and literature, a work of continuing fascination to anyone interested in understanding America.

Andrew S. Trees holds a Ph.D. in American History from the University of Virginia. He has taught at Rutgers University, Rhodes College, and the University of Virginia, and he is the author of *The Founding Fathers and the Politics of Character* (Princeton University Press).

CHAPTER I

I have ever had a pleasure in obtaining any little anecdotes of my ancestors. You may remember the inquiries I made among the remains of my relations when you were with me in England, and the journey I undertook for that purpose. Imagining it may be equally agreeable to you to learn the circumstances of *my* life, many of which you are unacquainted with, and expecting the enjoyment of a few weeks' uninterrupted leisure, I sit down to write them. Besides, there are some other inducements that excite me to this undertaking. From the poverty and obscurity in which I was born and in which I passed my earliest years, I have raised myself to a state of affluence and some degree of celebrity in the world. As constant good fortune has accompanied me even to an advanced period of life, my posterity will perhaps be desirous of learning the means which I employed, and which, thanks to Providence, so well succeeded with me. They may also deem them fit to be imitated, should any of them find themselves in similar circumstances.

This good fortune, when I reflect on it (which is frequently the case), has induced me sometimes to say that if it were left to my choice I should have no objection to go over the same life from its beginning to the end; requesting only the advantage authors have of correcting in a second edition the faults of the first. So would I also wish to change some incidents of it for others more favorable. Notwithstanding, if this condition was denied I should still accept the offer recommencing the same life. But as this repetition is not to be expected, that which resembles most living one's life over again seems to be to recall all the circumstances of it, and, to render this remembrance more durable, to record them in writing.

In thus employing myself, I shall yield to the inclination, so natural to old men, of talking of themselves and their own actions; and I shall indulge it without being tiresome to those who, from respect to my age, might conceive themselves obliged to listen to me, since they will be always free to read me or not. And lastly (I may as well confess it, as the denial of it would be believed by nobody), I shall, perhaps, not a little gratify my own vanity. Indeed, I never heard or saw the introductory words, "Without vanity I may say," etc., but some vain thing immediately followed. Most people dislike vanity in others, whatever share they have of it themselves; but I give it fair quarter wherever I meet with it, being persuaded that it is often productive of good to the possessor and to others who are within his sphere of action; and therefore, in many cases, it would not be altogether absurd if a man were to thank God for his *vanity* among the other comforts of life.

And now I speak of thanking God, I desire with all humility to acknowledge that I attribute the mentioned happiness of my past life to his divine providence, which led me to the means I used and gave the success. My belief of this induces me to *hope,* though I must not *presume,* that the same goodness will still be exercised toward me in continuing that happiness or enabling me to bear a fatal reverse, which I may experience as others have done; the complexion of my future fortune being known to Him only in whose power it is to bless us, even in our afflictions.

Some notes which one of my uncles, who had the same curiosity in collecting family anecdotes, once put into my hands, furnished me with several particulars relative to our ancestors. From these notes I learned that they lived in the same village, Ecton, in Northamptonshire, on a freehold of about thirty acres, for at least three hundred years, and how much longer could not be ascertained.

This small estate would not have sufficed for their maintenance without the business of a smith which had continued in the family down to my uncle's time, the eldest son being always brought up to that employment; a custom which he and my father followed with regard to their eldest sons. When I searched the registers at Ecton I found an account of their marriages and burials from the year 1555 only, as the registers kept did not commence previous thereto. I, however, learned from it that I was the youngest son of the youngest son for five generations back. My grandfather, Thomas, who was born in 1598, lived at Ecton till he was too old to continue his business, when he retired to Banbury, in Oxfordshire, to the house of his son John, with whom my father served an apprenticeship. There my uncle died and lies buried. We saw his grave-stone in 1758. His eldest son Thomas lived in the house at Ecton, and left it, with the land, to his only daughter, who, with her husband, one Fisher, of Wellingborough, sold it to Mr. Isted, now lord of the manor there. My grandfather had four sons, who grew up, viz., Thomas, John, Benjamin, and Josiah. Being at a distance from my papers, I will give you what account I can of them from memory; and if my papers are not lost in my absence, you will find among them many more particulars.

Thomas, my oldest uncle, was bred a smith under his father, but being ingenious and encouraged in learning, as all his brothers were, by an Esquire Palmer, then the principal inhabitant of that parish, he qualified himself for the bar and became a considerable man in the county; was chief mover of all public-spirited enterprises for the county or town of Northampton, as well as of his own village, of which many instances were related of him; and he was much taken notice of and patronized by Lord Halifax. He died in 1702, the 6th of January, four years to a day before I was born. The recital which some elderly persons made to us of his character I remember struck you as something extraordinary, from its similarity with what you knew of me. "Had he died," said you, "four years later on the same day, one might have supposed a transmigration."

John, my next uncle, was bred a dyer, I believe of wool. Benjamin was bred a silk-dyer, serving an apprenticeship in London. He was an ingenious man. I remember when I was a boy he came to my father's in Boston and resided in the house with us for several years. There was always a particular affection between my father and him, and I was his godson. He lived to a great age. He left behind him two quarto volumes of manuscript of his own poetry, consisting of fugitive pieces addressed to his friends. He had invented a short-hand of his own, which he taught me; but not having practiced it I have now forgotten it. He was very pious and an assiduous attendant at the sermons of the best preachers, which he reduced to writing according to his method, and had thus collected several volumes of them.

He was also a good deal of a politician; too much so, perhaps, for his station. There fell lately into my hands, in London, a collection he had made of all the principal political pamphlets relating to public affairs from the year 1641 to 1717. Many of the volumes are wanting, as appears by their numbering; but there still remain eight volumes in folio and twenty in quarto and in octavo. A dealer in old books had met with them, and knowing me by name, having bought books of him, he brought them to me. It would appear that my uncle must have left them here when he went to America, which was about fifty years ago. I found several of his notes in the margins. His grandson, Samuel Franklin, is still living in Boston.

Our humble family early embraced the reformed religion. Our forefathers continued Protestants through the reign of Mary, when they were sometimes in danger of persecution on account of their zeal against popery. They had an English Bible, and to conceal it and place it in safety, it was fastened open with tapes under and within the cover of a joint stool. When my great-grandfather wished to read it to his family, he placed the joint stool on his knees and then turned over the leaves under the tapes. One of the children stood at the door to give notice if he saw the apparitor coming, who was an officer of the spiritual court. In that case the stool was turned down again upon its feet, when the Bible remained concealed under it as before. This anecdote I had from Uncle Benjamin. The family continued all of the Church of England till about the end of Charles the Second's reign, when some of the ministers that had been ousted for their non-conformity, holding conventicles in Northamptonshire, my Uncle Benjamin and my father Josiah adhered to them, and so continued all their lives. The rest of the family remained with the Episcopal Church.

My father married young, and carried his wife, with three children, to New England about 1685. The conventicles being at that time forbidden by law and frequently disturbed in the meetings, some considerable men of his acquaintances determined to go to that country, and he was prevailed with to accompany them thither, where they expected to enjoy the exercise of their religion with freedom. By the same wife my father had four children more born there, and by a second ten others — in all seventeen; of whom I remember to have seen thirteen sitting together at his table, who all grew up to years of maturity and were married. I was the youngest son and the youngest of all the children except two daughters. I was born in Boston, in New England. My mother, the second wife of my father, was Abiah Folger, daughter of Peter Folger, one of the first settlers of New England, of whom honorable mention is made by Cotton Mather in his ecclesiastical history of that country, entitled *Magnalia Christi Americana,* as "a godly and learned Englishman," if I remember the words rightly. I was informed he wrote several small occasional works, but only one of them was printed, which I remember to have seen several years since. It was written in 1675. It was in familiar verse, according to the taste of the times and people, and addressed to the government there. It asserts the liberty of conscience in behalf of the Anabaptist, the Quakers, and other sectaries that had been persecuted. He attributes to this persecution the Indian wars and other calamities that had befallen the country, regarding them as so many judgments of God to punish so heinous an offense and exhorting the repeal of those laws, so contrary to charity. This piece appeared to me as written with manly freedom and a pleasing simplicity. The six lines I remember, but have forgotten the preceding ones of the stanza; the purport of them was that his censures proceeded from good will, and therefore he would be known to be the author:

> "Because to be a libeler
>   I hate it with my heart.
> From Sherbon Town[1] where now I dwell,
>   My name I do put here;
> Without offense your real friend,
>   It is Peter Folger."

My elder brothers were all put apprentices to different trades. I was put to the grammar school at eight years of age, my father intending to devote me as the tithe of his sons to the service of the Church. My early readiness in learning to read, which must have been very early, as I do not remember when I could not read, and the opinion of all his friends that I should certainly make a good scholar, encouraged him in this purpose of his. My Uncle Benjamin, too, approved of it, and proposed to give me his short-hand volumes of sermons to set up with if I would learn his short-hand. I continued, however, at the grammar school rather less than a year, though in that time I had risen gradually from the middle of the class of that year to be at the head of the same class, and was removed into the next class, whence I was to be placed in the third at the end of the year.

But my father, burdened with a numerous family, was unable, without inconvenience, to support the expense of a college education. Considering, moreover, as he said to one of his friends in my presence, the little encouragement that line of life afforded to those educated for it, he gave up his first intentions, took me from the grammar school, and sent me to a school for writing and arithmetic, kept by a then famous man, Mr. George Brownwell. He was a skillful master and succeeded in his profession, employing the mildest and most encouraging methods. Under him I learned to write a good hand pretty soon, but I failed entirely in arithmetic. At ten years old I was taken to help my father in his business, which was that of a tallow-chandler and soap-boiler; a business to which he was not bred, but had assumed on his arrival in New England, because he found that his dyeing trade, being in little request, would not maintain his family. Accordingly I was employed in cutting wicks for the candles, filling the molds for cast candles, attending the shop, going of errands, etc.

I disliked the trade and had a strong inclination to go to sea, but my father declared against it. But residing near the water I was much in it and on it I learned to swim well and to manage boats, and when embarked with other boys I was commonly allowed to govern, especially in any case of difficulty; and upon other occasions I was generally the leader among the boys, and sometimes led them into scrapes, of which I will mention one instance, as it shows an early projecting public spirit, though not then justly conducted. There was a salt marsh which bounded part of the mill-pond on the edge of which, at high water, we used to stand to fish for minnows. By much trampling we had made it a mere quagmire. My proposal was to build a wharf there for us to stand upon, and I showed my comrades a large heap of stones which were intended for a new house near the marsh and which would very well suit our purpose. Accordingly in the evening, when the workmen were gone home, I assembled a number of my playfellows, and we worked diligently like so many emmets, sometimes two or three to a stone, till we brought them all to make our little wharf. The next morning the workmen were surprised at missing the stones, which had formed our wharf. Inquiry was made after the authors of this transfer; we were discovered, complained of, and corrected by our fathers; and though I demonstrated the utility of our work, mine convinced me that that which was not honest could not be truly useful.

I suppose you may like to know what kind of a man my father was. He had an excellent constitution, was of a middle stature, well set, and very strong. He could draw prettily and was skilled a little in music. His voice was sonorous and agreeable, so that when he played on his violin and sung withal, as he was accustomed to do after the business of the day was over, it was extremely agreeable to hear. He had some knowledge of mechanics, and on occasion was very handy with other tradesmen's tools. But his great excellence was his sound understanding and his solid judgment in prudential matters, both in private and public affairs. It is true he was never employed in the latter, the numerous family he had to educate and the straitness of his circumstances keeping him close to his trade, but I remember well his being frequently visited by leading men, who consulted him for his opinion in public affairs and those of the church he belonged to, showing a great respect for his judgment and advice.

He was also much consulted by private persons about their affairs when any difficulty occurred, and frequently chosen an arbitrator between contending parties. At his table he liked to have, as often as he could, some sensible friend or neighbor to converse with, and always took care to start some ingenious or useful topic for discourse which might tend to improve the minds of his children. By this means he turned our attention to what was good, just, and prudent in the conduct of life, and little or no notice was ever taken of what related to the victuals on the table, whether it was well or ill dressed, in or out of season, of good or bad flavor, preferable or inferior to this or that other thing of the kind; so that I was brought up in such a perfect inattention to those matters as to be quite indifferent what kind of food was set before me. Indeed, I am so unobservant of it that to this day I can scarce tell a few hours after dinner of what dishes it consisted. This has been a great convenience to me in traveling, where my companions have been sometimes very unhappy for want of a suitable gratification of their more delicate, because better instructed, tastes and appetites.

My mother had likewise an excellent constitution; she suckled all her ten children. I never knew either my father or mother to have any sickness but that of which they died; he at eighty-nine and she at eighty-five years of age. They lie buried together at Boston, where I some years since placed a marble over their grave with this inscription:

JOSIAH FRANKLIN
and
ABIAH his wife,
Lie here interred.
They lived lovingly together in wedlock,
Fifty-five years;
And without an estate or any gainful employment,
By constant labor, and honest industry,
(With God's blessing,)
Maintained a large family comfortably;
And brought up thirteen children and seven grandchildren
Reputably.
From this instance, Reader,
Be encouraged to diligence in thy calling,
And distrust not Providence.
He was a pious and prudent man,
She a discreet and virtuous woman.
Their youngest son,
In filial regard to their memory,
Places this stone.
J. F. born 1655; died 1744. Æt. 89.
A. F. born 1667; died 1752. Æt. 85.

By my rambling digressions I perceive myself to be grown old. I used to write more methodically. But one does not dress for private company as for a public ball. Perhaps it is only negligence.

To return: I continued thus employed in my father's business for two years, that is, till I was twelve years old; and my brother John, who was bred to that business, having left my father, married and set up for himself at Rhode Island, there was every appearance that I was destined to supply his place and become a tallow-chandler. But my dislike to the trade continuing, my father had apprehensions that if he did not put me to one more agreeable I should break loose and go to sea, as my brother Josiah had done, to his great vexation. In consequence, he took me to walk with him and see joiners, bricklayers, turners, braziers, etc., at their work, that he might observe my inclination and endeavor to fix it on some trade or profession that would keep me on land. It has ever since been a pleasure to me to see good workmen handle their tools. And it has been often useful to me to have learned so much by it as to be able to do some trifling jobs in the house when a workman was not at hand, and to construct little machines for my experiments at the moment when the intention of making these was warm in my mind. My father determined at last for the cutler's trade, and placed me for some days on trial with Samuel, son to my Uncle Benjamin, who was bred to that trade in London and had just established himself in Boston. But the sum he exacted as a fee for my apprenticeship displeased my father, and I was taken home again.

From my infancy I was passionately fond of reading, and all the money that came into my hands was laid out in the purchasing of books. I was very fond of voyages. My first acquisition was Bunyan's works in separate little volumes. I afterward sold them to enable me to buy R. Burton's *Historical Collections.* They were small chapmen's books,[2] and cheap, forty volumes in all. My father's little library consisted chiefly of books in polemic divinity, most of which I read. I have often regretted that at a time when I had such a thirst for knowledge more proper books had not fallen in my way, since it was resolved I should not be bred to divinity. There was among them Plutarch's *Lives,* which I read abundantly, and I still think that time spent to great advantage. There was also a book of Defoe's, called *An Essay on Projects,* and another of Dr. Mather's, called *An Essay to Do Good,* which perhaps gave me a turn of thinking that had an influence on some of the principal future events of my life.

This bookish inclination at length determined my father to make me a printer, although he had already one son, James, of that profession. In 1717 my brother James returned from England, with a press and letters, to set up his business in Boston. I liked it much better than that of my father, but still had a hankering for the sea. To prevent the apprehended effect of such an inclination, my father was impatient to have me bound to my brother. I stood out some time, but at last was persuaded and signed the indenture when I was yet but twelve years old. I was to serve an apprenticeship till I was twenty-one years of age, only I was to be allowed journeyman's wages during the last year. In a little time I made a great progress in the business and became a useful hand to my brother. I now had access to better books. An acquaintance with the apprentices of booksellers enabled me sometimes to borrow a small one, which I was careful to return soon and clean. Often I sat up in my chamber reading the greatest part of the night when the book was borrowed in the evening and to be returned in the morning, lest it should be found missing.

After some time a merchant, an ingenious, sensible man, Mr. Matthew Adams, who had a pretty collection of books, frequented our printing-office, took notice of me, and invited me to see his library and very kindly proposed to loan me such books as I chose to read. I now took a strong inclination for poetry and wrote some little pieces. My brother, supposing it might turn to account, encouraged me and induced me to compose two occasional ballads. One was called *The Light-House Tragedy,* and contained an account of the shipwreck of Captain Worthilake with his two daughters; the other was a sailor's song, on the taking of the famous Teach, or "Blackbeard," the pirate. They were wretched stuff, in street-ballad style; and when they were printed my brother sent me about the town to sell them. The first sold prodigiously, the event being recent and having made a great noise. This success flattered my vanity; but my father discouraged me by criticising my performances and telling me verse-makers were generally beggars. Thus I escaped being a poet, and probably a very bad one; but as prose-writing had been of great use to me in the course of my life and was a principal means of my advancement, I shall tell you how in such a situation I acquired what little ability I may be supposed to have in that way.

There was another bookish lad in the town, John Collins by name, with whom I was intimately acquainted. We sometimes disputed, and very fond we were of argument and very desirous of confuting one another; which disputatious turn, by the way, is apt to become a very bad habit, making people often extremely disagreeable in company by the contradiction that is necessary to bring it into practice, and thence besides souring and spoiling the conversation, it is productive of disgusts, and perhaps enmities, with those who may have occasion for friendship. I had caught this by reading my father's books of dispute on religion. Persons of good sense, I have since observed, seldom fall into it, except lawyers, university men, and generally men of all sorts who have been bred at Edinburgh.

A question was once, somehow or other, started between Collins and me on the propriety of educating the female sex in learning and their abilities for study. He was of opinion that it was improper and that they were naturally unequal to it. I took the contrary side, perhaps a little for dispute's sake. He was naturally more eloquent, having a greater plenty of words, and sometimes, as I thought, I was vanquished more by his fluency than by the strength of his reasons. As we parted without settling the point and were not to see one another again for some time, I sat down to put my arguments in writing, which I copied fair and sent to him. He answered and I replied. Three or four letters on a side had passed, when my father happened to find my papers and read them. Without entering into the subject in dispute, he took occasion to talk to me about my manner of writing; observed that though I had the advantage of my antagonist in correct spelling and pointing (which he attributed to the printing house), I fell far short in elegance of expression, in method, and in perspicuity, of which he convinced me by several instances. I saw the justice of his remarks, and thence grew more attentive to my manner of writing and determined to endeavor to improve my style. At this time I met with an odd volume of the *Spectator.* I had never before seen any of them. I bought it, read it over and over, and was much delighted with it. I thought the writing excellent, and wished if possible to imitate it. With that view I took some of the papers, and making short hints of the sentiments in each sentence, laid them by a few days, and then, without looking at the book, tried to complete the papers again, by expressing each hinted sentiment at length, and as fully as it had been expressed before, in any suitable words that should occur to me. Then I compared my "Spectator" with the original, discovered some of my faults, and corrected them. But I found I wanted a stock of words or a readiness in recollecting and using them, which I thought I should have acquired before that time if I had gone on making verses; since the continual search for words of the same import, but of different length to suit the measure or of different sound for the rhyme, would have laid me under a constant necessity of searching for variety, and also have tended to fix that variety in my mind and make me master of it. Therefore I took some of the tales in the "Spectator" and turned them into verse; and after a time, when I had pretty well forgotten the prose, turned them back again.

I also sometimes jumbled my collection of hints into confusion, and after some weeks endeavored to reduce them into the best order before I began to form the full sentences and complete the subject. This was to teach me method in the arrangement of the thoughts. By comparing my work with the original, I discovered many faults and corrected them; but I sometimes had the pleasure to fancy that in certain particulars of small consequence I had been fortunate enough to improve the method or the language, and this encouraged me to think that I might in time come to be a tolerable English writer, of which I was extremely ambitious. The time I allotted for writing exercises and for reading was at night, or before work began in the morning, or on Sundays, when I contrived to be in the printing-house, avoiding as much as I could the constant attendance at public worship which my father used to exact of me when I was under his care, and which I still continued to consider a duty, though I could not afford time to practice it.

When about sixteen years of age I happened to meet with a book, written by one Tryon, recommending a vegetable diet. I determined to go into it. My brother being yet unmarried did not keep house, but boarded himself and his apprentices in another family. My refusing to eat flesh occasioned an inconvenience, and I was frequently chid for my singularity. I made myself acquainted with Tryon's manner of preparing some of his dishes, such as boiling potatoes or rice, making hasty-pudding and a few others, and then proposed to my brother that if he would give me weekly half the money he paid for board, I would board myself. He instantly agreed to it, and I presently found that I could save half what he paid me. This was an additional fund for buying of books; but I had another advantage in it. My brother and the rest going from the printing-house to their meals, I remained there alone, and dispatching presently my light repast (which was often no more than a biscuit or a slice of bread, a handful of raisins or a tart from the pastry-cook's, and a glass of water), had the rest of the time till their return for study; in which I made the greater progress from that greater clearness of head and quicker apprehension which generally attend temperance in eating and drinking. Now it was that (being on some occasion made ashamed of my ignorance in figures, which I had twice failed learning when at school) I took Cocker's book on *Arithmetic,* and went through the whole by myself with the greatest ease. I also read Seller's and Sturny's book on *Navigation,* which made me acquainted with the little geometry it contains; but I never proceeded far in that science. I read about this time Locke *On Human Understanding* and *The Art of Thinking,* by Messrs. de Port-Royal.

While I was intent on improving my language I met with an English grammar (I think it was Greenwood's) having at the end of it two little sketches on the arts of rhetoric and logic, the latter finishing with a dispute in the Socratic method; and soon after I procured Xenophon's *Memorable Things of Socrates,* wherein there are many examples of the same method. I was charmed with it, adopted it, dropped my abrupt contradictions and positive argumentation, and put on the humble inquirer. And being then, from reading Shaftesbury and Collins, made a doubter, as I already was in many points of our religious doctrines, I found this method the safest for myself and very embarrassing to those against whom I used it; therefore I took delight in it, practiced it continually, and grew very artful and expert in drawing people even of superior knowledge into concessions the consequence of which they did not foresee, entangling them in difficulties out of which they could not extricate themselves, and so obtaining victories that neither myself nor my cause always deserved.

I continued this method some few years, but gradually left it, retaining only the habit of expressing myself in terms of modest diffidence, never using, when I advanced anything that may possibly be disputed, the words *certainly, undoubtedly,* or any others that give the air of positiveness to an opinion; but rather say, *I conceive* or *apprehend* a thing to be so and so; *It appears to me,* or, *I should not think it, so or so, for such and such reasons;* or, *I imagine it to be so;* or, *It is so, if I am not mistaken.* This habit, I believe, has been of great advantage to me when I have had occasion to inculcate my opinions and persuade men into measures that I have been from time to time engaged in promoting. And as the chief ends of conversation are to *inform* or to *be informed,* to *please* or to *persuade,* I wish well-meaning and sensible men would not lessen their power of doing good by a positive assuming manner that seldom fails to disgust, tends to create opposition, and to defeat most of those purposes for which speech was given to us. In fact, if you wish to instruct others, a positive dogmatical manner in advancing your sentiments may occasion opposition and prevent a candid attention. If you desire instruction and improvement from others, you should not at the same time express yourself fixed in your present opinions. Modest and sensible men, who do not love disputation, will leave you undisturbed in the possession of your errors. In adopting such a manner, you can seldom expect to please your hearers or obtain the concurrence you desire. Pope judiciously observes —

"Men must be taught as if you taught them not,
And things unknown proposed as things forgot."

He also commended it to us

"To speak, though sure, with seeming diffidence."

And he might have joined with this line that which he has coupled with another, I think, less properly—

"For want of modesty is want of sense."

If you ask, Why less properly? I must repeat the lines,

"Immodest words admit of no defense,
"For want of modesty is want of sense."

Now, is not the *want of sense,* where a man is so unfortunate as to want it, some apology for his *want of modesty?* And would not the lines stand more justly thus?

"Immodest words admit *but* this defense,
That want of modesty is want of sense."

This, however, I should submit to better judgments.

My brother had, in 1720 or 1721, begun to print a newspaper. It was the second that appeared in America and was called the *New England Courant.* The only one before it was the Boston *News-Letter.* I remember his being dissuaded by some of his friends from the undertaking as not likely to succeed, one newspaper being in their judgment enough for America. At this time, 1771, there are not less than twenty-five. He went on, however, with the undertaking. I was employed to carry the papers to the customers after having worked in composing the types and printing off the sheets.

He had some ingenious men among his friends, who amused themselves by writing little pieces for this paper, which gained it credit and made it more in demand, and these gentlemen often visited us. Hearing their conversations and their accounts of the approbation their papers were received with, I was excited to try my hand among them. But being still a boy, and suspecting that my brother would object to printing anything of mine in his paper if he knew it to be mine, I contrived to disguise my hand, and writing an anonymous paper, I put it at night under the door of the printing-house. It was found in the morning and communicated to his writing friends when they called in as usual. They read it, commented on it in my hearing, and I had the exquisite pleasure of finding it met with their approbation, and that in their different guesses at the author none were named but men of some character among us for learning and ingenuity. I suppose that I was rather lucky in my judges, and that they were not really so very good as I then believed them to be. Encouraged, however, by this attempt, I wrote and sent in the same way to the press several other pieces that were equally approved; and I kept my secret till all my fund of sense for such performances was exhausted, and then discovered it, when I began to be considered a little more by my brother's acquaintance.

However, that did not quite please him, as he thought it tended to make me too vain. This might be one occasion of the differences we began to have about this time. Though a brother, he considered himself as my master and me as his apprentice, and accordingly expected the same services from me as he would from another, while I thought he degraded me too much in some he required of me, who from a brother expected more indulgence. Our disputes were often brought before our father, and I fancy I was either generally in the right or else a better pleader, because the judgment was generally in my favor. But my brother was passionate and had often beaten me, which I took extremely amiss; and thinking my apprenticeship very tedious, I was continually wishing for some opportunity of shortening it, which at length offered in a manner unexpected. Perhaps this harsh and tyrannical treatment of me might be a means of impressing me with the aversion to arbitrary power that has stuck to me through my whole life.

One of the pieces in our newspaper on some political point, which I have now forgotten, gave offense to the Assembly. He was taken up, censured, and imprisoned for a month by the Speaker's warrant, I suppose because he would not discover the author. I, too, was taken up and examined before the Council; but though I did not give them any satisfaction, they contented themselves with admonishing me, and dismissed me, considering me perhaps as an apprentice who was bound to keep his master's secrets. During my brother's confinement, which I resented a good deal, notwithstanding our private differences, I had the management of the paper; and I made bold to give our rulers some rubs in it, which my brother took very kindly, while others began to consider me in an unfavorable light as a youth who had a turn for libeling and satire.

My brother's discharge was accompanied with an order, and a very odd one, that "James Franklin should no longer print the newspaper called the *New England Courant.*" On a consultation held in our printing-office among his friends what he should do in this conjuncture, it was proposed to elude the order by changing the name of the paper. But my brother, seeing inconveniences in this, came to a conclusion, as a better way, to let the paper in future be printed in the name of Benjamin Franklin; and in order to avoid the censure of the Assembly, that might fall on him as still printing it by his apprentice, he contrived and consented that my old indenture should be returned to me with a discharge on the back of it, to show in case of necessity; and in order to secure to him the benefit of my service, I should sign new indentures for the remainder of my time, which were to be kept private. A very flimsy scheme it was; however, it was immediately executed, and the paper was printed accordingly, under my name, for several months.

At length, a fresh difference arising between my brother and me, I took upon me to assert my freedom, presuming that he would not venture to produce the new indentures. It was not fair in me to take this advantage, and this I therefore reckon one of the first *errata* of my life; but the unfairness of it weighed little with me when under the impressions of resentment for the blows his passion too often urged him to bestow upon me. Though he was otherwise not an ill-natured man; perhaps I was too saucy and provoking.

When he found I would leave him, he took care to prevent my getting employment in any other printing-house of the town by going round and speaking to every master, who accordingly refused to give me work. I then thought of going to New York, as the nearest place where there was a printer. And I was rather inclined to leave Boston when I reflected that I had already made myself a little obnoxious to the governing party, and from the arbitrary proceedings of the Assembly in my brother's case, it was likely I might, if I stayed, soon bring myself into scrapes; and further, that my indiscreet disputations about religion began to make me pointed at with horror by good people as an infidel and atheist. I concluded, therefore, to remove to New York; but my father now siding with my brother, I was sensible that if I attempted to go openly means would be used to prevent me. My friend Collins, therefore, undertook to manage my flight. He agreed with the captain of a New York sloop to take me, under pretense of my being a young man of his acquaintance that had an intrigue with a girl of bad character, whose parents would compel me to marry her, and that I could neither appear nor come away publicly. I sold my books to raise a little money, was taken on board the sloop privately, had a fair wind, and in three days found myself at New York, near three hundred miles from my home, at the age of seventeen (October 1723), without the least recommendation or knowledge of any person in the place, and very little money in my pocket.

CHAPTER II

THE inclination I had had for the sea was by this time done away, or I might now have gratified it. But having another profession and conceiving myself a pretty good workman, I offered my services to a printer of the place, old Mr. William Bradford, who had been the first printer in Pennsylvania, but had removed thence in consequence of a quarrel with the governor, George Keith. He could give me no employment, having little to do and hands enough already; but he said, "My son at Philadelphia has lately lost his principal hand, Aquila Rose, by death; if you go thither I believe he may employ you." Philadelphia was one hundred miles further. I set out, however, in a boat for Amboy, leaving my chest and things to follow me round by sea.

In crossing the bay we met with a squall that tore our rotten sails to pieces, preventing our getting into the Kill, and drove us upon Long Island. In our way a drunken Dutchman, who was a passenger too, fell overboard; when he was sinking I reached through the water to his shock pate and drew him up, so that we got him in again. His ducking sobered him a little and he went to sleep, taking first out of his pocket a book, which he desired I would dry for him. It proved to be my old favorite author, Bunyan's *Pilgrim's Progress,* in Dutch, finely printed on good paper, copper cuts, a dress better than I had ever seen it wear in its own language. I have since found that it has been translated into most of the languages of Europe, and suppose it has been more generally read than any other book, except perhaps the

Bible. Honest John was the first that I know of who mixed narration and dialogue: a method of writing very engaging to the reader, who in the most interesting parts finds himself, as it were, admitted into the company and present at the conversation. Defoe has imitated him successfully in his *Robinson Crusoe*, in his *Moll Flanders,* and other pieces; and Richardson has done the same in his *Pamela,* etc.

On approaching the island we found it was in a place where there could be no landing, there being a great surge on the stony beach. So we dropped anchor and swung out our cable toward the shore. Some people came down to the shore and hallooed to us, as we did to them; but the wind was so high and the surge so loud that we could not understand each other. There were some small boats near the shore, and we made signs and called to them to fetch us; but they either did not comprehend us or it was impracticable, so they went off. Night approaching, we had no remedy but to have patience till the wind abated, and in the meantime the boatmen and myself concluded to sleep if we could; and so we crowded into the hatches, where we joined the Dutchman, who was still wet, and the spray, breaking over the head of our boat, leaked through to us, so that we were soon almost as wet as he. In this manner we lay all night, with very little rest; but the wind abating the next day, we made a shift to reach Amboy before night, having been thirty hours on the water, without victuals or any drink but a bottle of filthy rum, the water we sailed on being salt.

In the evening I found myself very feverish and went to bed; but having read somewhere that cold water drunk plentifully was good for fever, I followed the prescription and sweat plentifully most of the night. My fever left me, and in the morning, crossing the ferry, I proceeded on my journey on foot, having fifty miles to go to Burlington, where I was told I should find boats that would carry me the rest of the way to Philadelphia.

It rained very hard all the day; I was thoroughly soaked, and by noon a good deal tired; so I stopped at a poor inn, where I stayed all night, beginning now to wish I had never left home. I made so miserable a figure, too, that I found, by the questions asked me, I was suspected to be some runaway indentured servant and in danger of being taken up on that suspicion. However, I proceeded next day and got in the evening to an inn within eight or ten miles of Burlington, kept by one Dr. Brown. He entered into conversation with me while I took some refreshment, and finding I had read a little, became very obliging and friendly. Our acquaintance continued all the rest of his life. He had been, I imagine, an ambulatory quack doctor, for there was no town in England nor any country in Europe of which he could not give a very particular account. He had some letters, and was ingenious, but he was an infidel, and wickedly undertook, some years after, to turn the Bible into doggerel verse, as Cotton had formerly done with Virgil. By this means he set many facts in a ridiculous light, and might have done mischief with weak minds if his work had been published; but it never was.

At his house I lay that night, and arrived the next morning at Burlington, but had the mortification to find that the regular boats were gone a little before, and no other expected to go before Tuesday, this being Saturday. Wherefore I returned to an old woman in the town, of whom I had bought some gingerbread to eat on the water, and asked her advice. She proposed to lodge me till a passage by some other boat occurred. I accepted her offer, being much fatigued by traveling on foot. Understanding I was a printer, she would have had me remain in that town and follow my business, being ignorant what stock was necessary to begin with. She was very hospitable, gave me a dinner of ox-cheek with great good-will, accepting only of a pot of ale in return; and I thought myself fixed till Tuesday should come. However, walking in the evening by the side of the river, a boat came by, which I found was going toward Philadelphia with several people in her. They took me in, and as there was no wind we rowed all the way; and about midnight, not having yet seen the city, some of the company were confident we must have passed it and would row no further; the others knew not where we were, so we put toward the shore, got into a creek, landed near an old fence, with the rails of which we made a fire, the night being cold, in October, and there we remained till daylight. Then one of the company knew the place to be Cooper's Creek, a little above Philadelphia, which we saw as soon as we got out of the creek, and arrived there about eight or nine o'clock on the Sunday morning and landed at Market Street wharf.

I have been the more particular in this description of my journey, and shall be so of my first entry into that city, that you may in your mind compare such unlikely beginnings with the figure I have since made there. I was in my working dress, my best clothes coming round by sea. I was dirty, from my being so long in the boat. My pockets were stuffed out with shirts and stockings, and I knew no one nor where to look for lodging. Fatigued with walking, rowing, and the want of sleep, I was very hungry; and my whole stock of cash consisted in a single dollar, and about a shilling in copper coin, which I gave to the boatmen for my passage. At first they refused it, on account of my having rowed; but I insisted on their taking it. Man is sometimes more generous when he has little money than when he has plenty; perhaps to prevent his being thought to have but little.

I walked toward the top of the street, gazing about till near Market Street, when I met a boy with bread. I had often made a meal of dry bread, and inquiring where he had bought it, I went immediately to the baker's he directed me to. I asked for biscuits, meaning such as we had at Boston; that sort, it seems, was not made at Philadelphia. I then asked for a threepenny loaf and was told they had none. Not knowing the different prices nor the names of the different sorts of bread, I told him to give me threepenny worth of any sort. He gave me accordingly three great puffy rolls. I was surprised at the quantity, but took it, and having no room in my pockets, walked off with a roll under each arm and eating the other. Thus I went up Market Street as far as Fourth Street, passing by the door of Mr. Read, my future wife's father; when she, standing at the door, saw me, and thought I made, as I certainly did, a most awkward, ridiculous appearance. Then I turned and went down Chestnut Street and part of Walnut Street, eating my roll all the way; and coming round found myself again at Market Street wharf, near the boat I came in, to which I went for a draught of the river water; and being filled with one of my rolls, gave the other two to a woman and her child that came down the river in the boat with us and were waiting to go further.

Thus refreshed I walked again up the street, which by this time had many clean-dressed people in it, who were all walking the same way. I joined them, and thereby was led into the great meeting-house of the Quakers, near the market. I sat down among them, and after looking round a while and hearing nothing said, being very drowsy through labor and want of rest the preceding night, I fell fast asleep and continued so till the meeting broke up, when some one was kind enough to rouse me. This, therefore, was the first house I was in, or slept in, in Philadelphia.

I then walked down toward the river, and looking in the face of every one, I met a young Quaker man whose countenance pleased me, and accosting him requested he would tell me where a stranger could get a lodging. We were then near the sign of the Three Mariners. "Here," said he, "is a house where they receive strangers; but it is not a reputable one. If thee wilt walk with me I'll show thee a better one," and he conducted me to the Crooked Billet, in Water Street. There I got a dinner, and while I was eating several questions were asked me, as from my youth and appearance I was suspected of being a runaway.

After dinner, my host having shown me to a bed, I laid myself on it without undressing and slept till six in the evening, when I was called to supper. I went to bed again very early and slept very soundly till next morning. Then I dressed myself as neat as I could and went to Andrew Bradford, the printer's. I found in the shop the old man his father, whom I had seen at New York, and who, traveling on horseback, had got to Philadelphia before me. He introduced me to his son, who received me civilly, gave me a breakfast, but told me he did not at present want a hand, being lately supplied with one; but there was another printer in town, lately set up, one Keimer, who perhaps might employ me; if not, I should be welcome to lodge at his house, and he would give me a little work to do now and then till fuller business should offer.

The old gentleman said he would go with me to the new printer; and when we found him, "Neighbor," said Bradford, "I have brought to see you a young man of your business: perhaps you may want such a one." He asked me a few questions, put a composing-stick in my hand to see how I worked, and then said he would employ me soon, though he had just then nothing for me to do. And taking old Bradford, whom he had never seen before, to be one of the townspeople that had a good-will for him, entered into a conversation on his present undertaking and prospects; while Bradford, not discovering that he was the other printer's father, on Keimer's saying he expected soon to get the greatest part of the business in his own hands, drew him on, by artful questions and starting little doubts, to explain all his views, what influence he relied on, and in what manner he intended to proceed. I, who stood by and heard all, saw immediately that one was a crafty old sophister and the other a true novice. Bradford left me with Keimer, who was greatly surprised when I told him who the old man was.

The printing-house, I found, consisted of an old damaged press and a small, worn-out font of English types, which he was using himself, composing an "Elegy" on Aquila Rose, before mentioned; an ingenious young man, of excellent character, much respected in the town, secretary to the Assembly, and a pretty poet. Keimer made verses too, but very indifferently. He could not be said to *write* them, for his method was to compose them in the types directly out of his head. There being no copy, but one pair of cases, and the "Elegy" probably requiring all the letters, no one could help him. I endeavored to put his press (which he had not yet used and of which he understood nothing) into order to be worked with; and promising to come and print off his "Elegy" as soon as he should have got it ready, I returned to Bradford's, who gave me a little job to do for the present, and there I lodged and dieted. A few days after Keimer sent for me to print off the "Elegy." And now had got another pair of cases and a pamphlet to reprint, on which he set me to work.

These two printers I found poorly qualified for their business. Bradford had not been bred to it and was very illiterate, and Keimer, though something of a scholar, was a mere compositor, knowing nothing of press-work. He had been one of the French prophets and could act their enthusiastic agitations. At this time he did not profess any particular religion, but something of all on occasion; was very ignorant of the world, and had, as I afterward found, a good deal of the knave in his composition. He did not like my lodging at Bradford's while I worked with him. He had a house, indeed, but without furniture, so he could not lodge me; but he got me a lodging at Mr. Read's, before mentioned, who was the owner of his house; and my chest of clothes being come by this time, I made rather a more respectable appearance in the eyes of Miss Read than I had done when she first happened to see me eating my roll in the street.

I began now to have some acquaintance among the young people of the town that were lovers of reading, with whom I spent my evenings very pleasantly, and gained money by my industry and frugality. I lived very contented and forgot Boston as much as I could, and did not wish to be known where I resided except to my friend Collins, who was in the secret and kept it faithfully. At length, however, an incident happened that occasioned my return home much sooner than I had intended. I had a brother-in-law, Robert Holmes, master of a sloop that traded between Boston and Delaware. He being at Newcastle, forty miles below Philadelphia, and hearing of me, wrote me a letter mentioning the grief of my relations and friends in Boston at my abrupt departure, assuring me of their good-will to me, and that everything would be accommodated to my mind if I would return, to which he entreated me earnestly. I wrote an answer to his letter, thanked him for his advice, but stated my reasons for quitting Boston so fully and in such a light as to convince him that I was not so much in the wrong as he had apprehended.

Sir William Keith, governor of the province, was then at Newcastle, and Captain Holmes, happening to be in company with him when my letter came to hand, spoke to him of me and showed him the letter. The governor read it and seemed surprised when he was told my age. He said I appeared a young man of promising parts and therefore should be encouraged; the printers at Philadelphia were wretched ones, and if I would set up there he made no doubt I should succeed; for his part he would procure me the public business and do me every other service in his power. This my brother-in-law Holmes afterward told me in Boston, but I knew as yet nothing of it; when one day Keimer and I, being at work together near the window, we saw the governor and another gentleman (who proved to be Colonel French, of Newcastle, in the province of Delaware), finely dressed, come directly across the street to our house, and heard them at the door.

Keimer ran down immediately, thinking it a visit to him; but the governor inquired for me, came up, and with a condescension and politeness I had been quite unused to made him many compliments, desired to be acquainted with me, blamed me kindly for not having made myself known to him when I first came to the place, and would have me away with him to the tavern, where he was going with Colonel French to taste, as he said, some excellent Madeira. I was not a little surprised and Keimer stared with astonishment. I went, however, with the governor and Colonel French to a tavern at the corner of Third Street, and over the Madeira he proposed my setting up my business. He stated the probabilities of my success, and both he and Colonel French assured me I should have their interest and influence to obtain for me the public business of both governments. And as I expressed doubts that my father would assist me in it, Sir William said he would give me a letter to him, in which he would set forth the advantages, and he did not doubt he should determine him to comply. So it was concluded I should return to Boston by the first vessel, with the governor's letter to my father. In the mean time it was to be kept a secret, and I went on working with Keimer as usual. The governor sent for me now and then to dine with him, which I considered a great honor, more particularly as he conversed with me in a most affable, familiar, and friendly manner.

About the end of April, 1724, a little vessel offered for Boston. I took leave of Keimer as going to see my friends. The governor gave me an ample letter, saying many flattering things of me to my father and strongly recommending the project of my setting up at Philadelphia as a thing that would make my fortune. We struck on a shoal in going down the bay and sprung a leak; we had a blustering time at sea and were obliged to pump almost continually, at which I took my turn. We arrived safe, however, at Boston in about a fortnight. I had been absent seven months, and my friends had heard nothing of me, for my brother James was not yet returned and had not written about me. My unexpected appearance surprised the family; all were, however, very glad to see me and made me welcome except my brother. I went to see him at his printing-house. I was better dressed than ever while in his service, having a genteel new suit from head to foot, a watch, and my pockets lined with near five pounds sterling in silver. He received me not very frankly, looked me all over, and turned to his work again.

The journeymen were inquisitive where I had been, what sort of a country it was, and how I liked it. I praised it much and the happy life I led in it, expressing strongly my intention of returning to it; and one of them asking what kind of money we had there, I produced a handful of silver and spread it before them, which was a kind of *raree-show* they had not been used to, paper being the money of Boston. Then I took an opportunity of letting them see my watch; and lastly (my brother still grum and sullen) gave them a dollar to drink and took my leave. This visit of mine offended him extremely. For when my mother some time after spoke to him of a reconciliation and of her wish to see us on good terms together, and that we might live for the future as brothers, he said I had insulted him in such a manner before his people that he could never forget or forgive it. In this, however, he was mistaken.

My father received the governor's letter with some surprise, but said little of it to me for some time. Captain Holmes returning, he showed it to him and asked him if he knew Sir William Keith, and what kind of a man he was; adding that he must be of small discretion to think of setting a youth up in business who wanted three years to arrive at man's estate. Holmes said what he could in favor of the project, but my father was decidedly against it and at last gave a flat denial. He wrote a civil letter to Sir William, thanking him for the patronage he had so kindly offered me, and declined to assist me as yet in setting up, I being, in his opinion, too young to be trusted with the management of an undertaking so important, and for which the preparation required a considerable expenditure.

My *old* companion Collins, who was a clerk in the post-office, pleased with the account I gave him of my new country, determined to go thither also; and while I waited for my father's determination, he set out before me by land to Rhode Island, leaving his books, which were a pretty collection in mathematics and natural philosophy, to come with mine and me to New York, where he proposed to wait for me.

My father, though he did not approve Sir William's proposition, was yet pleased that I had been able to obtain so advantageous a character from a person of such note where I had resided, and that I had been so industrious and careful as to equip myself so handsomely in so short a time; therefore, seeing no prospect of an accommodation between my brother and me, he gave his consent to my returning again to Philadelphia, advised me to behave respectfully to the people there, endeavor to obtain the general esteem and avoid lampooning and libeling, to which he thought I had too much inclination; telling me that by steady industry and prudent parsimony I might save enough by the time I was twenty-one to set me up, and that if I came near the matter he would help me out with the rest. This was all I could obtain, except some small gifts as tokens of his and my mother's love, when I embarked again for New York, now with their approbation and their blessing.

The sloop putting in at Newport, Rhode Island, I visited my brother John, who had been married and settled there some years. He received me very affectionately, for he always loved me. A friend of his, one Vernon, having some money due to him in Pennsylvania, about thirty-five pounds currency, desired I would recover it for him and keep it till I had his directions what to employ it in. Accordingly he gave me an order to receive it. This business afterward occasioned me a good deal of uneasiness.

At Newport we took in a number of passengers, among whom were two young women traveling together and a sensible, matron-like Quaker lady, with her servants. I had shown an obliging disposition to render her some little services, which probably impressed her with sentiments of good-will toward me, for when she witnessed the daily growing familiarity between the young women and myself, which they appeared to encourage, she took me aside and said: "Young man, I am concerned for thee, as thou hast no friend with thee and seems not to know much of the world or of the snares youth is exposed to. Depend upon it, these are very bad women: I can see it by all their actions; and if thee art not upon thy guard they will draw thee into some danger; they are strangers to thee, and I advise thee, in a friendly concern for thy welfare, to have no acquaintance with them." As I seemed at first not to think so ill of them as she did, she mentioned some things she had observed and heard that had escaped my notice, but now convinced me she was right. I thanked her for her kind advice and promised to follow it. When we arrived at New York they told me where they lived and invited me to come and see them, but I avoided it; and it was well I did, for the next day the captain missed a silver spoon and some other things that had been taken out of his cabin, and knowing that these were a couple of strumpets, he got a warrant to search their lodgings, found the stolen goods, and had the thieves punished. So though we had escaped a sunken rock, which we scraped upon in the passage, I thought this escape of rather more importance to me.

At New York I found my friend Collins, who had arrived there some time before me. We had been intimate from children and had read the same books together, but he had the advantage of more time for reading and studying and a wonderful genius for mathematical learning, in which he far outstripped me. While I lived in Boston, most of my hours of leisure for conversation were spent with him, and he continued a sober as well as industrious lad, was much respected for his learning by several of the clergy and other gentlemen, and seemed to promise making a good fig-ure in life. But during my absence he had acquired a habit of drinking brandy, and I found by his own account, as well as that of others, that he had been drunk every day since his arrival at New York, and behaved himself in a very extravagant manner. He had gamed, too, and lost his money, so that I was obliged to discharge his lodgings and defray his expenses on the road and at Philadelphia, which proved a great burden to me.

The then Governor of New York, Burnet (son of Bishop Burnet), hearing from the captain that one of the passengers had a great many books on board, desired him to bring me to see him. I waited on him, and should have taken Collins with me had he been sober. The governor received me with great civility, showed me his library, which was a considerable one, and we had a good deal of conversation relative to books and authors. This was the second governor who had done me the honor to take notice of me, and for a poor boy like me it was very pleasing.

We proceeded to Philadelphia. I received in the way Vernon's money, without which we could hardly have finished our journey. Collins wished to be employed in some counting-house; but whether they discovered his dram-drinking by his breath or by his behavior, though he had some recommendations he met with no success in any application, and continued lodging and boarding at the same house with me, and at my expense. Knowing I had that money of Vernon's he was continually borrowing of me, still promising repayment as soon as he should be in business. At length he had got so much of it that I was distressed to think what I should do in case of being called on to remit it.

His drinking continued, about which we sometimes quarreled, for when a little intoxicated he was very irritable. Once in a boat on the Delaware, with some other young men, he refused to row in his turn. "I will be rowed home," said he. "We will not row you," said I. "You must," said he, "or stay all night on the water, just as you please." The others said, "Let us row; what signifies it?" But, my mind being soured with his other conduct, I continued to refuse. So he swore he would make me row or throw me overboard; and coming along stepping on the thwarts toward me, when he came up and struck at me, I clapped my head under his thighs and, rising, pitched him headforemost into the river. I knew he was a good swimmer and so was under little concern about him; but before he could get round to lay hold of the boat we had with a few strokes pulled her out of his reach, and whenever he drew near the boat we asked him if he would row, striking a few strokes to slide her away from him. He was ready to stifle with vexation and obstinately would not promise to row. Finding him at last beginning to tire, we drew him into the boat and brought him home dripping wet. We hardly exchanged a civil word after this adventure. At length a West India captain, who had a commission to procure a preceptor for the sons of a gentleman at Barbadoes, met with him and proposed to carry him thither to fill that situation. He accepted, and promised to remit me what he owed me out of the first money he should receive, but I never heard of him after.

The violation of my trust respecting Vernon's money was one of the first great *errata* of my life; and this showed that my father was not much out in his judgment when he considered me as too young to manage business. But Sir William, on reading his letter, said he was too prudent—that there was a great difference in persons, and discretion did not always accompany years, nor was youth always without it. "But since he will not set you up I will do it myself. Give me an inventory of the things necessary to be had from England and I will send for them. You shall repay me when you are able. I am resolved to have a good printer here, and I am sure you must succeed." This was spoken with such an appearance of cordiality that I had not the least doubt of his meaning what he said. I had hitherto kept the proposition of my setting up a secret in Philadelphia, and I still kept it. Had it been known that I depended on the governor, probably some friend that knew him better would have advised me not to rely on him, as I afterward heard it as his known character to be liberal of promises which he never meant to keep. Yet, unsolicited as he was by me, how could I think his generous offers insincere? I believed him one of the best men in the world.

I presented him an inventory of a little printing-house, amounting, by my computation, to about one hundred pounds sterling. He liked it, but asked me if my being on the spot in England to choose the types and see that everything was good of the kind might not be of some advantage. "Then," said he, "when there you may make acquaintance and establish correspondences in the book-selling and stationery line." I agreed that this might be advantageous. "Then," said he, "get yourself ready to go by the Annis," which was the annual ship, and the only one, at that time usually passing between London and Philadelphia. But as it would be some months before the Annis sailed I continued working with Keimer, fretting extremely about the money Collins had got from me and in great apprehensions of being called upon for it by Vernon; this, however, did not happen for some years after.

I believe I have omitted mentioning that in my first voyage from Boston to Philadelphia, being becalmed off Block Island, our crew employed themselves in catching cod, and hauled up a great number. Till then I had stuck to my resolution to eat nothing that had had life; and on this occasion I considered, according to my master Tryon, the taking of every fish as a kind of unprovoked murder, since none of them had done or could do us any injury that might justify this massacre. All this seemed very reasonable. But I had been formerly a great lover of fish, and when it came out of the frying-pan it smelled admirably well. I balanced some time between principle and inclination, till, recollecting that when the fish were opened I saw smaller fish taken out of their stomachs, then, thought I, "If you eat one another I don't see why we may not eat you"; so I dined upon cod very heartily, and have since continued to eat as other people, returning only now and then occasionally to a vegetable diet. So convenient a thing it is to be a *reasonable creature*, since it enables one to find or make a *reason* for everything one has a mind to do.

Keimer and I lived on a pretty good familiar footing and agreed tolerably well, for he suspected nothing of my setting up. He retained a great deal of his old enthusiasm and loved argumentation; we therefore had many disputations. I used to work him so with my Socratic method, and had trepanned him so often by questions apparently so distant from any point we had in hand, yet by degrees leading to the point and bringing him into difficulties and contradictions, that at last he grew ridiculously cautious, and would hardly answer me the most common question without asking first, "What do you intend to infer from that?" However, it gave him so high an opinion of my abilities in the confuting way that he seriously proposed my being his colleague in a project he had of setting up a new sect. He was to preach the doctrines and I was to confound all opponents. When he came to explain with me upon the doctrines I found several conundrums, which I objected to unless I might have my way a little too and introduce some of mine.

Keimer wore his beard at full length, because somewhere in the Mosiac law it is said, *"Thou shalt not mar the corners of thy beard."* He likewise kept the seventh day, Sabbath; and these two points were essential with him. I disliked both, but agreed to them on condition of his adopting the doctrine of not using animal food. "I doubt," said he, "my constitution will not bear it." I assured him it would and that he would be the better for it. He was usually a great eater, and I wished to give myself some diversion in half-starving him. He consented to try the practice if I would keep him company. I did so, and we held it for three months. Our provisions were purchased, cooked, and brought to us regularly by a woman in the neighborhood, who had from me a list of forty dishes which she prepared for us at different times, in which there entered neither fish, flesh, nor fowl. This whim suited me the better at this time from the cheapness of it, not costing us above eighteen pence sterling each per week. I have since kept several Lents most strictly, leaving the common diet for that, and that for the common, abruptly, without the least inconvenience; so that I think there is little in the advice of making those changes by easy gradations. I went on pleasantly, but poor Keimer suffered grievously, grew tired of the project, longed for the flesh-pots of Egypt, and ordered a roast pig. He invited me and two women friends to dine with him, but, it being brought too soon upon table, he could not resist the temptation and ate the whole before we came.

I had made some courtship during this time to Miss Read. I had a great respect and affection for her, and had some reasons to believe she had the same for me; but as I was about to take a long voyage and we were both very young, only a little above eighteen, it was thought most prudent by her mother to prevent our going too far at present, as a marriage, if it were to take place, would be more convenient after my return, when I should be, as I hoped, set up in my business. Perhaps, too, she thought my expectations not so well founded as I imagined them to be.

My chief acquaintances at this time were Charles Osborne, Joseph Watson, and James Ralph, all lovers of reading. The two first were clerks to an eminent scrivener or conveyancer in the town, Charles Brockden. The other was a clerk to a merchant. Watson was a pious, sensible young man of great integrity; the others rather more lax in their principles of religion, particularly Ralph, who, as well as Collins, had been unsettled by me, for which they both made me suffer. Osborne was sensible, candid, frank, sincere, and affectionate to his friends, but in literary matters too fond of criticism. Ralph was ingenious, genteel in his manners, and extremely eloquent. I think I never knew a prettier talker. Both were great admirers of poetry and began to try their hands in little pieces. Many pleasant walks we have had together on Sundays in the woods on the banks of the Schuylkill, where we read to one another and conferred on what we had read.

Ralph was inclined to give himself up entirely to poetry, not doubting that he might make great proficiency in it and even make his fortune by it. He pretended that the greatest poets must, when they first began to write, have committed as many faults as he did. Osborne endeavored to dissuade him, assured him he had no genius for poetry, and advised him to think of nothing beyond the business he was bred to; that in the mercantile way, though he had no stock, he might by his diligence and punctuality recommend himself to employment as a factor and in time acquire wherewith to trade on his own account. I approved for my part the amusing one's self with poetry now and then, so far as to improve one's language, but no further.

On this it was proposed that we should each of us, at our next meeting, produce a piece of our own composing, in order to improve by our mutual observations, criticisms, and corrections. As language and expression were what we had in view, we excluded all considerations of invention by agreeing that the task should be a version of the eighteenth psalm, which describes the descent of a Deity. When the time of our meeting drew nigh, Ralph called on me first and let me know his piece was ready. I told him I had been busy, and having little inclination had done nothing. He then showed me his piece for my opinion, and I much approved it, as it appeared to me to have great merit. "Now," said he, "Osborne never will allow the least merit in anything of mine, but makes a thousand criticisms out of mere envy. He is not so jealous of you. I wish, therefore, you would take this piece and produce it as yours. I will pretend not to have had time and so produce nothing. We shall then hear what he will say to it." It was agreed, and I immediately transcribed it, that it might appear in my own hand.

We met. Watson's performance was read; there were some beauties in it, but many defects. Osborne's was read; it was much better. Ralph did it justice; remarked some faults, but applauded the beauties. He himself had nothing to produce. I was backward, seemed desirous of being excused, had not had sufficient time to correct, etc. But no excuse could be admitted; produce I must. It was read and repeated. Watson and Osborne gave up the contest and joined in applauding it. Ralph only made some criticisms and proposed some amendments; but I defended my text. Osborne was severe against Ralph and told me he was no better able to criticise than compose verses. As these two were returning home, Osborne expressed himself still more strongly in favor of what he thought my production, having before refrained, as he said, lest I should think he meant to flatter me. "But who would have imagined," said he, "that Franklin was capable of such a performance; such painting, such force, such fire! He has even improved on the original. In common conversation he seems to have no choice of words; he hesitates and blunders, and yet, good God, how he writes!" When we next met, Ralph discovered the trick we had played and Osborne was laughed at.

This transaction fixed Ralph in his resolution of becoming a poet. I did all I could to persuade him from it, but he continued scribbling verses till Pope cured him. He became, however, a pretty good prose-writer. More of him hereafter. But as I may not have occasion to mention the other two, I shall just remark here that Watson died in my arms a few years after, much lamented, being the best of our set. Osborne went to the West Indies, where he became an eminent lawyer and made money, but died young. He and I had made a serious agreement that the one who happened first to die should, if possible, make a friendly visit to the other and acquaint him how he found things in that separate state. But he never fulfilled his promise.

The governor, seeming to like my company, had me frequently at his house, and his setting me up was always mentioned as a fixed thing. I was to take with me letters recommendatory to a number of his friends, besides the letter of credit to furnish me with the necessary money for purchasing the press, types, paper, etc. For these letters I was appointed to call at different times, when they were to be ready; but a future time was still named. Thus we went on till the ship—whose departure, too, had been several times postponed—was on the point of sailing. Then when I called to take my leave and receive the letters, his secretary, Dr. Baird, came out to me and said the governor was extremely busy in writing, but would be down at Newcastle before the ship, and then the letters would be delivered to me.

Ralph, though married and having one child, had determined to accompany me in this voyage. It was thought he intended to establish a correspondence and obtain goods to sell on commission; but I found after that having some cause of discontent with his wife's relations, he proposed to leave her on their hands and never return to America. Having taken leave of my friends and exchanged promises with Miss Read, I quitted Philadelphia in the ship, which anchored at Newcastle. The governor was there, but when I went to his lodging his secretary came to me from him with expressions of the greatest regret that he could not then see me, being engaged in business of the utmost importance, but that he would send the letters to me on board, wishing me heartily a good voyage and a speedy return, etc. I returned on board a little puzzled, but still not doubting.

CHAPTER III

MR. Andrew Hamilton, a celebrated lawyer of Philadelphia, had taken his passage in the same ship for himself and son, with Mr. Denham, a Quaker merchant, and Messrs. Oniam and Russel, masters of an iron works in Maryland, who had engaged the great cabin; so that Ralph and I were forced to take up with a berth in the steerage, and none on board knowing us, were considered as ordinary persons. But Mr. Hamilton and his son (it was James, since governor) returned from Newcastle to Philadelphia, the father being recalled by a great fee to plead for a seized ship. And just before we sailed Colonel French coming on board and showing me great respect I was more taken notice of, and, with my friend Ralph, invited by the other gentlemen to come into the cabin, there being now room. Accordingly we removed thither.

Understanding that Colonel French had brought on board the governor's dispatches, I asked the captain for those letters that were to be under my care. He said all were put into the bag together and he could not then come at them, but before we landed in England I should have an opportunity of picking them out; so I was satisfied for the present and we proceeded on our voyage. We had a sociable company in the cabin and lived uncommonly well, having the addition of all Mr. Hamilton's stores, who had laid in plentifully. In this passage Mr. Denham contracted a friendship for me that continued during his life. The voyage was otherwise not a pleasant one, as we had a great deal of bad weather.

When we came into the Channel, the captain kept his word with me and gave me an opportunity of examining the bag for the governor's letters. I found some upon which my name was put as under my care. I picked out six or seven that by the handwriting I thought might be the promised letters, especially as one of them was addressed to Baskett, the king's printer, and another to some stationer. We arrived in London the 24th December, 1724. I waited upon the stationer, who came first in my way, delivering the letter as from Governor Keith. "I don't know such a person," said he; but opening the letter, "Oh, this is from Riddlesden. I have lately found him to be a complete rascal, and I will have nothing to do with him nor receive any letters from him." So putting the letter into my hand, he turned on his heel and left me to serve some customer. I was surprised to find these were not the governor's letters, and after recollecting and comparing circumstances, I began to doubt his sincerity. I found my friend Denham and opened the whole affair to him. He let me into Keith's character, told me there was not the least probability that he had written any letters for me; that no one who knew him had the smallest dependence on him; and he laughed at the idea of the governor's giving me a letter of credit, having, as he said, no credit to give. On my expressing some concern about what I should do, he advised me to endeavor getting some employment in the way of my business. "Among the printers here," said he, "you will improve yourself, and when you return to America you will set up to greater advantage."

We both of us happened to know, as well as the stationer, that Riddlesden, the attorney, was a very knave. He had half-ruined Miss Read's father by persuading him to be bound for him. By this letter it appeared there was a secret scheme on foot to the prejudice of Mr. Hamilton (supposed to be then coming over with us); that Keith was concerned in it with Riddlesden. Denham, who was a friend of Hamilton's, thought he ought to be acquainted with it; so when he arrived in England, which was soon after, partly from resentment and ill-will to Keith and Riddlesden and partly from good-will to him, I waited on him and gave him the letter. He thanked me cordially, the information being of importance to him, and from that time he became my friend, greatly to my advantage afterward on many occasions.

But what shall we think of a governor playing such pitiful tricks and imposing so grossly on a poor, ignorant boy! It was a habit he had acquired. He wished to please everybody, and having little to give he gave expectations. He was otherwise an ingenious, sensible man, a pretty good writer, and a good governor for the people, though not for his constituents, the proprietaries, whose instructions he sometimes disregarded. Several of our best laws were of his planning and passed during his administration.

Ralph and I were inseparable companions. We took lodgings together in Little Britain at three shillings and sixpence a week, as much as we could then afford. He found some relations, but they were poor and unable to assist him. He now let me know his intentions of remaining in London and that he never meant to return to Philadelphia. He had brought no money with him, the whole he could muster having been expended in paying his passage. I had fifteen pistoles, so he borrowed occasionally of me to subsist while he was looking out for business. He first endeavored to get into the play-house, believing himself qualified for an actor; but Wilkes[1], to whom he applied, advised him candidly not to think of that employment, as it was impossible he should succeed in it. Then he proposed to Roberts, a publisher in Paternoster Row, to write for him a weekly paper like the *Spectator*, on certain conditions, which Roberts did not approve. Then he endeavored to get employment as a hackney writer, to copy for the stationers and lawyers about the Temple, but could not find a vacancy.

For myself, I immediately got into work at Palmer's, a famous printing-house in Bartholomew Close, where I continued near a year. I was pretty diligent, but I spent with Ralph a good deal of my earnings at plays and public amusements. We had nearly consumed all my pistoles, and now just rubbed on from hand to mouth. He seemed quite to have forgotten his wife and child, and I by degrees my engagements with Miss Read, to whom I never wrote more than one letter, and that was to let her know I was not likely soon to return. This was another of the great *errata* of my life, which I could wish to correct if I were to live it over again. In fact, by our expenses I was constantly kept unable to pay my passage.

At Palmer's I was employed in composing for the second edition of Wollaston's *Religion of Nature*. Some of his reasonings not appearing to me well founded, I wrote a little metaphysical piece in which I made remarks on them. It was entitled A *Dissertation on Liberty and Necessity, Pleasure and Pain*. I inscribed it to my friend Ralph; I printed a small number. It occasioned my being more considered by Mr. Palmer as a young man of some ingenuity, though he seriously expostulated with me upon the principles of my pamphlet, which to him appeared abominable. My printing this pamphlet was another *erratum*. While I lodged in Little Britain I made an acquaintance with one Wilcox, a bookseller, whose shop was next door. He had an immense collection of second-hand books. Circulating libraries were not then in use, but we agreed that on certain reasonable terms, which I now have forgotten, I might take, read, and return any of his books. This I esteemed a great advantage, and I made as much use of it as I could.

My pamphlet by some means falling into the hands of one Lyons, a surgeon, author of a book entitled *The Infallibility of Human Judgment*, it occasioned an acquaintance between us. He took great notice of me, called on me often to converse on those subjects, carried me to the Horns, a pale-ale-house in —Lane, Cheapside, and introduced me to Dr. Mandeville, author of the *Fable of the Bees*, who had a club there, of which he was the soul; being a most facetious, entertaining companion. Lyons too introduced me to Dr. Pemberton, at Batson's coffee-house, who promised to give me an opportunity, some time or other, of seeing Sir Isaac Newton, of which I was extremely desirous; but this never happened.

I had brought over a few curiosities, among which the principal was a purse made of the *asbestos,* which purifies by fire. Sir Hans Sloane heard of it, came to see me, and invited me to his house in Bloomsbury Square, showed me all his curiosities, and persuaded me to add that to the number; for which he paid me handsomely.

In our house lodged a young woman, a milliner, who I think had a shop in the Cloisters. She had been genteelly bred, was sensible, lively, and of a most pleasing conversation. Ralph read plays to her in the evenings, they grew intimate, she took another lodging, and he followed her. They lived together some time; but he being still out of business and her income not sufficient to maintain them with her child, he took a resolution of going to London to try for a country school, which he thought himself well qualified to undertake, as he wrote an excellent hand and was a master of arithmetic and accounts. This, however, he deemed a business below him, and confident of future better fortune, when he should be unwilling to have it known that he was once so meanly employed, he changed his name and did me the honor to assume mine; for I soon after had a letter from him, acquainting me that he was settled in a small village (in Berkshire, I think it was, where he taught reading and writing to ten or a dozen boys at sixpence each per week), recommending Mrs. T——to my care and desiring me to write to him, directing for *Mr. Franklin,* schoolmaster, at such a place.

He continued to write to me frequently, sending me large specimens of an epic poem which he was then composing, and desiring my remarks and corrections. These I gave him from time to time, but endeavored rather to discourage his proceeding. One of Young's Satires was then just published. I copied and sent him a great part of it, which set in a strong light the folly of pursuing the Muses. All was in vain; sheets of the poem continued to come by every post. In the mean time, Mrs. T——, having on his account lost her friends and business, was often in distresses, and used to send for me and borrow what money I could spare to help to alleviate them. I grew fond of her company, and being at that time under no religious restraint, and taking advantage of my importance to her, I attempted to take some liberties with her (another *erratum*), which she repulsed, with a proper degree of resentment. She wrote to Ralph and acquainted him with my conduct; this occasioned a breach between us; and when he returned to London he let me know he considered all the obligations he had been under to me as annulled; from which I concluded I was never to expect his repaying the money I had lent him or that I had advanced for him. This, however, was of little consequence, as he was totally unable, and by the loss of his friendship I found myself relieved from a heavy burden. I now began to think of getting a little beforehand, and, expecting better employment, I left Palmer's to work at Watt's, near Lincoln's Inn Fields, a still greater printing-house. Here I continued all the rest of my stay in London.

At my first admission into the printing-house I took to working at press, imagining I felt a want of bodily exercise I had been used to in America, where press work is mixed with the composing. I drank only water; the other workmen, near fifty in number, were great drinkers of beer. On occasion I carried up and down stairs a large form of type in each hand, when others carried but one in both hands. They wondered to see, from this and several instances, that the *Water-American,* as they called me, was *stronger* than themselves, who drank *strong* beer! We had an ale-house boy, who attended always in the house to supply the workmen. My companion at the press drank every day a pint before breakfast, a pint at breakfast with his bread and cheese, a pint between breakfast and dinner, a pint at dinner, a pint in the afternoon about six o'clock, and another pint when he had done his day's work. I thought it a detestable custom; but it was necessary, he supposed, to drink *strong* beer that he might be *strong* to labor. I endeavored to convince him that the bodily strength afforded by beer could only be in proportion to the grain or flour of the barley dissolved in the water of which it was made; that there was more flour in a pennyworth of bread; and therefore if he could eat that with a pint of water it would give him more strength than a quart of beer. He drank on, however, and had four or five shillings to pay out of his wages every Saturday night for that vile liquor, an expense I was free from. And thus these poor devils keep themselves always under.

Watts, after some weeks, desiring to have me in the composing-room, I left the press-room; a new *bien venu* for drink, being five shillings, was demanded of me by the compositors. I thought it an imposition, as I had paid one to the pressman; the master thought so too and forbade my paying it. I stood out two or three weeks, was accordingly considered as an excommunicate, and had so many little pieces of private malice practiced on me, by mixing my sorts, transposing and breaking my matter, etc., etc., if ever I stepped out of the room, and all ascribed to the *chapel ghost,* which they said ever haunted those not regularly admitted, that notwith-standing the master's protection, I found myself obliged to com-ply and pay the money; convinced of the folly of being on ill-terms with those one is to live with continually.

I was now on a fair footing with them and soon acquired con-siderable influence. I proposed some reasonable alterations in the *chapel*[2] laws and carried them against all opposition. From my example a great many of them left their muddling breakfast of beer, bread, and cheese, finding they could with me be supplied from a neighboring house with a large porringer of hot-water gruel, sprinkled with pepper, crumbled with bread, and a bit of butter in it, for the price of a pint of beer, viz., three halfpence. This was a more comfortable as well as a cheaper breakfast and kept their heads clearer. Those who continued sotting with their beer all day were often, by not paying, out of credit at the ale-house, and used to make interest with me to get beer; their *light,* as they phrased it, *being out.* I watched the pay-table on Saturday night and collected what I stood engaged for them, having to pay sometimes near thirty shillings a week on their accounts. This, and my being estimated a pretty good *riggite,* that is, a jocular verbal satirist, supported my consequence in the society. My constant attendance (I never making a *St. Monday*) recommended me to the master, and my uncommon quickness at composing occasioned my being put upon work of dispatch, which was generally better paid. So I went on now very agreeably.

My lodgings in Little Britain being too remote, I found another in Duke Street, opposite to the Romish chapel. It was up three pair of stairs backward, at an Italian warehouse. A widow lady kept the house; she had a daughter, and a maid-servant, and a journeyman who attended the warehouse, but lodged abroad. After sending to inquire my character at the house where I last lodged, she agreed to take me in at the same rate—three shillings and sixpence a week; cheaper, as she said, from the protection she expected in having a man to lodge in the house. She was a widow, an elderly woman; had been bred a Protestant, being a clergyman's daughter, but was converted to the Catholic religion by her husband, whose memory she much revered; had lived much among people of distinction, and knew a thousand anecdotes of them as far back as the time of Charles II. She was lame in her knees with the gout and therefore seldom stirred out of her room, so sometimes wanted company; and hers was so highly amusing to me that I was sure to spend an evening with her whenever she desired it. Our supper was only half an anchovy each on a very little slice of bread and butter and half a pint of ale between us; but the entertainment was in her conversation. My always keeping good hours and giving little trouble in the family made her unwilling to part with me, so that when I talked of a lodging I had heard of, nearer my business, for two shillings a week (which, intent as I was on saving money, made some difference), she bid me not think of it, for she would abate me two shillings a week for the future; so I remained with her at one shilling and sixpence as long as I stayed in London.

In the garret of her house there lived a maiden lady of seventy, in the most retired manner, of whom my landlady gave me this account: that she was a Roman Catholic; had been sent abroad when young and lodged in a nunnery, with an intent of becoming a nun; but, the country not agreeing with her, she returned to

England, where, there being no nunnery, she had vowed to lead the life of a nun as near as might be done in those circumstances. Accordingly she had given all her estate to charitable purposes, reserving only twelve pounds a year to live on; and out of this sum she still gave a part in charity, living herself on water-gruel only and using no fire but to boil it. She had lived many years in that garret, being permitted to remain there gratis by successive Catholic tenants of the house below, as they deemed it a blessing to have her there. A priest visited her to confess her every day. "From this I asked her," said my landlady, "how she, as she lived, could possibly find so much employment for a confessor." "Oh!" said she, "it is impossible to avoid *vain thoughts.*" I was permitted once to visit her. She was cheerful and polite and conversed pleasantly. The room was clean, but had no other furniture than a mattress, a table with a crucifix and a book, a stool which she gave me to sit on, and a picture over the chimney of St. Veronica displaying her handkerchief, with the miraculous figure of Christ's bleeding face on it, which she explained to me with a great seriousness.

She looked pale, but was never sick; and I give it as another instance on how small an income life and health may be supported.

At Watt's printing-house I contracted an acquaintance with an ingenious young man, one Wygate, who, having wealthy relations, had been better educated than most printers; was a tolerable Latinist, spoke French, and loved reading. I taught him and a friend of his to swim at twice going into the river, and they soon became good swimmers. They introduced me to some gentlemen from the country, who went to Chelsea by water to see the college and Don Saltero's curiosities. In our return at the request of the company, whose curiosity Wygate had excited, I stripped and leaped into the river and swam from near Chelsea to Blackfriars; performing in the way many feats of activity, both upon and under the water, and surprised and pleased those to whom they were novelties.

I had from a child been delighted with this exercise, had studied and practiced Thevenot's motions and positions and added some of my own, aiming at the graceful and easy as well as the useful. All these I took this occasion of exhibiting to the company, and was much flattered by their admiration; and Wygate, who was desirous of becoming a master, grew more and more attached to me on that account, as well as from the similarity of our studies. He at length proposed to me traveling all over Europe together, supporting ourselves everywhere by working at our business. I was once inclined to it, but mentioning it to my good friend Mr. Denham, with whom I often spent an hour when I had leisure, he dissuaded me from it, advising me to think only of returning to Pennsylvania, which he was now about to do.

I must record one trait of this good man's character. He had formerly been in business at Bristol, but failed in debt to a number of people, compounded, and went to America. There, by a close application to business as a merchant, he acquired a plentiful fortune in a few years. Returning to England in the ship with me, he invited his old creditors to an entertainment, at which he thanked them for the easy composition they had favored him with; and when they expected nothing but the treat, every man, at the first remove, found under his plate an order on a banker for the amount of the unpaid remainder, with interest.

He now told me he was about to return to Philadelphia, and should carry over a great quantity of goods in order to open a store there. He proposed to take me over as his clerk, to keep his books — in which he would instruct me — copy his letters, and attend the store. He added that as soon as I should be acquainted with mercantile business he would promote me by sending me with a cargo of flour and bread to the West Indies, and procure me commissions from others which would be profitable, and if I managed well would establish me handsomely. The thing pleased me, for I was grown tired of London, remembered with pleasure the happy months I had spent in Pennsylvania, and wished again to see it. Therefore I immediately agreed, on the terms of fifty pounds a year, Pennsylvania money; less than my then present gettings as a compositor, but affording a better prospect.

I now took leave of printing, as I thought, forever, and was daily employed in my new business, going about with Mr. Denham among the tradesmen to purchase various articles and see them packed up, delivering messages, calling upon workmen to dispatch, etc.; and when all was on board I had a few days' leisure. On one of these days I was, to my surprise, sent for by a great man I knew only by name, Sir William Wyndham, and I waited upon him. He had heard, by some means or other, of my swimming from Chelsea to Blackfriars and of my teaching Wygate and another young man to swim in a few hours. He had two sons about to set out on their travels; he wished to have them first taught swimming, and proposed to gratify me handsomely if I would teach them. They were not yet come to town and my stay was uncertain, so I could not undertake it. But from the incident I thought it likely that if I were to remain in England and open a swimming-school I might get a good deal of money; and it struck me so strongly that had the overture been made me sooner, probably I should not so soon have returned to America. Many years after, you and I had something of more importance to do with one of these sons of Sir William Wyndham, become Earl of Egremont, which I shall mention in its place.

Thus I passed about eighteen months in London; most part of the time I worked hard at my business and spent but little upon myself, except in seeing plays and in books. My friend Ralph had kept me poor. He owed me about twenty-seven pounds, which I was now never likely to receive; a great sum out of my small earnings! I loved him, notwithstanding, for he had many amiable qualities. I had improved my knowledge, however, though I had by no means improved my fortune; but I had made some very ingenious acquaintance, whose conversation was of great advantage to me, and I had read considerably.

CHAPTER IV

WE sailed from Gravesend on the 23d of July, 1726. For the incidents of the voyage I refer you to my journal, where you will find them all minutely related. Perhaps the most important part of that journal is the *plan*[1] to be found in it, which I framed at sea, for regulating the future conduct of my life. It is the more remarkable as being formed when I was so young, and yet being pretty faithfully adhered to quite through to old age.

We landed at Philadelphia the 11th of October, where I found sundry alterations. Keith was no longer governor, being superseded by Major Gordon; I met him walking the streets as a common citizen. He seemed a little ashamed at seeing me and passed without saying anything. I should have been as much ashamed at seeing Miss Read had not her friends, despairing with reason of my return after the receipt of my letter, persuaded her to marry another, one Rogers, a potter, which was done in my absence. With him, however, she was never happy, and soon parted from him, refusing to cohabit with him or bear his name, it being now said he had another wife. He was a worthless fellow, though an excellent workman, which was the temptation to her friends. He got into debt, ran away in 1727 or 1728, went to the West Indies, and died there. Keimer had got a better house, a shop well supplied with stationery, plenty of new types, and a number of hands, though none good, and seemed to have a great deal of business.

Mr. Denham took a store in Water Street, where we opened our goods; I attended the business diligently, studied accounts, and grew in a little time expert at selling. We lodged and boarded together; he counseled me as a father, having a sincere regard for me. I respected and loved him, and we might have gone on together very happily, but in the beginning of February, 1727, when I had just passed my twenty-first year, we both were taken ill. My distemper was a pleurisy, which very nearly carried me off. I suffered a good deal, gave up the point in my own mind, and was at the time rather disappointed when I found myself recovering; regretting, in some degree, that I must now, some time or other, have all that disagreeable work to go over again. I forget what Mr. Denham's distemper was; it held him a long time and at length carried him off. He left me a small legacy in a nuncupative will as a token of his kindness for me, and he left me once more to the wide world; for the store was taken into the care of his executors and my employment under him ended.

My brother-in-law, Holmes, being now in Philadelphia, advised my return to my business; and Keimer tempted me, with an offer of large wages by the year, to come and take the management of his printing-house, that he might better attend to his stationer's shop. I had heard a bad character of him in London from his wife and her friends, and was not for having any more to do with him. I wished for employment as a merchant's clerk, but, not meeting with any, I closed again with Keimer. I found in his house these hands: Hugh Meredith, a Welsh Pennsylvanian, thirty years of age, bred to country work; he was honest, sensible, a man of experience, and fond of reading, but addicted to drinking. Stephen Potts, a young countryman of full age, bred to the same, of uncommon natural parts and great wit and humor, but a little idle. These he had agreed with at extreme low wages per week, to be raised a shilling every three months, as they would deserve by improving in their business; and the expectation of these high wages, to come on hereafter, was what he had drawn them in with. Meredith was to work at press; Potts at bookbinding, which he by agreement was to teach them, though he knew neither one nor the other; John —, a wild Irishman, brought up to no business, whose services for four years Keimer had purchased from the captain of a ship; he, too, was to be made a pressman; George Webb, an Oxford scholar, whose time for four years he had likewise bought, intending him for a compositor, of whom more presently; and David Harry, a country boy whom he had taken apprentice.

I soon perceived that the attention of engaging me at wages so much higher than he had been used to give was to have these raw cheap hands formed through me; and as soon as I had instructed them, they being all articled to him, he should be able to do without me. I went, however, very cheerfully, put his printing-house in order, which had been in great confusion, and brought his hands by degrees to mind their business and to do it better.

It was an odd thing to find an Oxford scholar in the situation of a bought servant. He was not more than eighteen years of age, and he gave me this account of himself: that he was born in Gloucester, educated at a grammar school, and had been distinguished among his scholars for some apparent superiority in performing his part when they exhibited plays; belonged to the Wits' Club there and had written some pieces in prose and verse, which were printed in the Gloucester newspapers. Thence was sent to Oxford; there he continued about a year, but not well satisfied, wishing of all things to see London and become a player. At length receiving his quarterly allowance of fifteen guineas, instead of discharging his debts he went out of town, hid his gown in a furze bush, and walked to London, where, having no friend to advise him, he fell into bad company, soon spent his guineas, found no means of being introduced among the players, grew necessitous, pawned his clothes, and wanted bread. Walking the street very hungry, not knowing what to do with himself, a crimp's bill was put into his hand offering immediate entertainment and encouragement to such as would bind themselves to serve in America. He went directly, signed the indentures, was put into the ship and came over, never writing a line to his friends to acquaint them what was become of him. He was lively, witty, good-natured, and a pleasant companion, but idle, thoughtless, and imprudent to the last degree.

John, the Irishman, soon ran away; with the rest I began to live very agreeably, for they all respected me the more as they found Keimer incapable of instructing them, and that from me they learned something daily. My acquaintance with ingenious people in the town increased. We never worked on Saturday, that being Keimer's Sabbath, so that I had two days for reading. Keimer himself treated me with great civility and apparent regard, and nothing now made me uneasy but my debt to Vernon, which I was yet unable to pay, being hitherto but a poor economist. He, however, kindly made no demand of it.

Our printing-house often wanted sorts, and there was no letter foundry in America. I had seen types cast at James' in London, but without much attention to the manner; however, I contrived a mold and made use of the letters we had as puncheons, struck the matrices in lead, and thus supplied in a pretty tolerable way all deficiencies. I also engraved several things on occasion; made the ink; I was warehouseman; and, in short, quite a *factotum*.

But however serviceable I might be, I found that my services became every day of less importance as the other hands improved in their business; and when Keimer paid me a second quarter's wages, he let me know that he felt them too heavy and thought I should make an abatement. He grew by degrees less civil, put on more the airs of master, frequently found fault, was captious, and seemed ready for an outbreaking. I went on nevertheless with a good deal of patience, thinking that his incumbered circumstances were partly the cause. At length a trifle snapped our connection; for, a great noise happening near the courthouse, I put my head out of the window to see what was the matter. Keimer, being in the street, looked up and saw me, called out to me in a loud voice and angry tone to mind my business, adding some reproachful words that nettled me the more for their publicity; all the neighbors who were looking out on the same occasion being witnesses how I was treated. He came up immediately into the printing-house; continued the quarrel, high words passed on both sides, he gave me the quarter's warning we had stipulated, expressing a wish that he had not been obliged to give so long a warning. I told him his wish was unnecessary, for I would leave him that instant; and so taking my hat walked out-of-doors, desiring Meredith, whom I saw below, to take care of some things I left and bring them to my lodgings.

Meredith came accordingly in the evening, when we talked my affair over. He had conceived a great regard for me and was very unwilling that I should leave the house while he remained in it. He dissuaded me from returning to my native country, which I began to think of; reminded me that Keimer was in debt for all he possessed; that his creditors began to be uneasy; that he kept his shop miserably, sold often without a profit for ready money, and often trusted without keeping accounts; that he must therefore fail, which would make a vacancy I might profit of. I objected my want of money. He then let me know that his father had a high opinion of me, and from some discourse that had passed between them he was sure would advance money to set me up if I would enter into partnership with him. "My time," said he, "will be out with Keimer in the spring; by that time we may have our press and types in from London. I am sensible I am no workman. If you like it your skill in the business will be set against the stock I furnish, and we will share the profits equally."

The proposal was agreeable to me and I consented; his father was in town and approved of it, the more as he said I had great influence with his son, had prevailed on him to abstain long from dram-drinking, and he hoped might break him of that wretched habit entirely when we came to be so closely connected. I gave an inventory to the father, who carried it to a merchant; the things were sent for, the secret was to be kept till they should arrive, and in the mean time I was to get work, if I could, at the other printing-house. But I found no vacancy there, and so remained idle a few days, when Keimer, on a prospect of being employed to print some paper money in New Jersey which would require cuts and various types that I only could supply, and apprehending Bradford might engage me and get the job from him, sent me a very civil message that old friends should not part for a few words, the effect of sudden passion, and wishing me to return. Meredith persuaded me to comply, as it would give more opportunity for his improvement under my daily instructions; so I returned, and we went on more smoothly than for some time before. The New Jersey job was obtained; I contrived a copperplate press for it, the first that had been seen in the country; I cut several ornaments and checks for the bills. We went together to Burlington, where I executed the whole to satisfaction, and he received so large a sum for the work as to be enabled thereby to keep himself longer from ruin.

At Burlington I made acquaintance with many principal people of the province. Several of them had been appointed by the Assembly a committee to attend the press and take care that no more bills were printed than the law directed. They were, therefore, by turns constantly with us, and generally he who attended brought with him a friend or two for company. My mind having been much more improved by reading than Keimer's, I suppose it was for that reason my conversation seemed to be more valued. They had me to their houses, introduced me to their friends, and showed me much civility; while he, though the master, was a little neglected. In truth, he was an odd creature, ignorant of common life, fond of rudely opposing received opinions, slovenly to extreme dirtiness, enthusiastic in some points of religion, and a little knavish withal.

We continued there near three months, and by that time I could reckon among my acquired friends Judge Allen, Samuel Bustill, the Secretary of the Province, Isaac Pearson, Joseph Cooper, and several of the Smiths, members of Assembly, and Isaac Decow, the Surveyor-General. The latter was a shrewd, sagacious old man, who told me that he began for himself, when young, by wheeling clay for the brickmakers; learned to write after

he was of age; carried the chain for surveyors, who taught him sur-
veying, and he had now, by his industry, acquired a good estate;
and said he, "I foresee that you will soon work this man out of his
business and make a fortune in it at Philadelphia." He had then
not the least intimation of my intention to set up there or any-
where. These friends were afterward of great use to me, as I occasionally was to some of them. They all continued their regard for
me as long as they lived.

Before I enter upon my public appearance in business, it may
be well to let you know the then state of my mind with regard to
my principles and morals, that you may see how far those influ-
enced the future events of my life. My parents had early given me
religious impressions and brought me through my childhood
piously in the Dissenting way. But I was scarce fifteen when, after
doubting by turns several points as I found them disputed in the
different books I read, I began to doubt of the Revelation itself.
Some books against deism fell into my hands; they were said to be
the substance of the sermons which had been preached at Boyle's
Lectures. It happened that they wrought an effect on me quite
contrary to what was intended by them. For the arguments of the
deists, which were quoted to be refuted, appeared to me much
stronger than the refutations; in short, I soon became a thorough
deist. My arguments perverted some others, particularly Collins
and Ralph, but each of those having wronged me greatly without
the least compunction, and recollecting Keith's conduct toward
me (who was another freethinker) and my own toward Vernon
and Miss Read, which at times gave me great trouble, I began to
suspect that this doctrine, though it might be true, was not very
useful. My London pamphlet, printed in 1725,[2] which had for its
motto these lines of Dryden:

> "Whatever is, is right. But purblind man
> Sees but a part o' the chain, the nearest links;
> His eyes not carrying to that equal beam,
> That poises all above,"

and which from the attributes of God, his infinite wisdom, goodness, and power, concluded that nothing could possibly be wrong in the world, and that vice and virtue were empty distinctions, no such things existing, appeared now not so clever a performance as I once thought it; and I doubted whether some error had not insinuated itself unperceived into my argument so as to infect all that followed, as is common in metaphysical reasonings.

I grew convinced that *truth, sincerity,* and *integrity,* in dealings between man and man, were of the utmost importance to the felicity of life; and I formed written resolutions, which still remain in my journal book, to practice them ever while I lived. Revelation had indeed no weight with me as such; but I entertained an opinion that though certain actions might not be bad *because* they were forbidden by it, or good *because* it commanded them, yet probably those actions might be forbidden *because* they were bad for us, or commanded *because* they were beneficial to us in their own natures, all the circumstances of things considered. And this persuasion, with the kind hand of Providence, or some guardian angel, or accidental favorable circumstances and situations, or all together, preserved me, through this dangerous time of youth and the hazardous situations I was sometimes in among strangers, remote from the eye and advice of my father, free from any *willful* gross immorality or injustice that might have been expected from my want of religion. I say *willful,* because the instances I have mentioned had something of *necessity* in them, from my youth, inexperience, and the knavery of others. I had therefore a tolerable character to begin in the world with. I valued it properly and determined to preserve it.

We had not been long returned to Philadelphia before the new types arrived from London. We settled with Keimer and left him by his consent before he heard of it. We found a house to let near the market and took it. To lessen the rent, which was then but twenty-four pounds a year, though I have since known it let for seventy, we took in Thomas Godfrey, a glazier, and his family, who were to pay a considerable part of it to us and we to board with them. We had scarce opened our letters and put our press in order, before George House, an acquaintance of mine, brought a countryman to us whom he had met in the street inquiring for a printer. All our cash was now expended in the variety of particulars we had been obliged to procure, and this countryman's five shillings, being our first-fruits and coming so seasonably, gave me more pleasure than any crown I have since earned; and the gratitude I felt toward House has made me often more ready than perhaps I otherwise should have been to assist young beginners.

There are croakers in every country, always boding its ruin. Such an one there lived in Philadelphia; a person of note, an elderly man with a wise look and a very grave manner of speaking; his name was Samuel Mickle. This gentleman, a stranger to me, stopped me one day at my door and asked me if I was the young man who had lately opened a new printing-house. Being answered in the affirmative, he said he was sorry for me, because it was an expensive undertaking and the expense would be lost; for Philadelphia was a sinking place, the people already half-bankrupts or near being so; all the appearances of the contrary, such as new buildings and the rise of rents, being to his certain knowledge fallacious, for they were in fact among the things that would ruin us. Then he gave me such a detail of misfortunes now existing or that were soon to exist that he left me half-melancholy. Had I known him before I engaged in this business, probably I never should have done it. This person continued to live in this decaying place and to declaim in the same strain, refusing for many years to buy a house there because all was going to destruction; and at last I had the pleasure of seeing him give five times as much for one as he might have bought it for when he first began croaking.

CHAPTER V

I should have mentioned before that in the autumn of the preceding year I had formed most of my ingenious acquaintance into a club for mutual improvement, which we called the Junto. We met on Friday evenings. The rules that I drew up required that every member in his turn should produce one or more queries on any point of morals, politics, or natural philosophy, to be discussed by the company; and once in three months produce and read an essay of his own writing on any subject he pleased. Our debates were to be under the direction of a president and to be conducted in the sincere spirit of inquiry after truth, without fondness for dispute or desire of victory; and to prevent warmth, all expressions of positiveness in opinions or direct contradiction were after some time made contraband and prohibited under small pecuniary penalties.

The first members were Joseph Breintnal, a copier of deeds for the scriveners, a good-natured, friendly, middle-aged man, a great lover of poetry, reading all he could meet with and writing some that was tolerable; very ingenious in making little knick-knackeries and of sensible conversation.

Thomas Godfrey, a self-taught mathematician, great in his way and afterward inventor of what is now called Hadley's quadrant.[1] But he knew little out of his way and was not a pleasing companion; as, like most great mathematicians I have met with, he expected universal precision in everything said, or was forever denying or distinguishing upon trifles, to the disturbance of all conversation. He soon left us.

Nicholas Scull, a surveyor, afterward surveyor-general, who loved books and sometimes made a few verses.

William Parsons, bred a shoemaker, but loving reading, had acquired a considerable share of mathematics, which he first studied with a view to astrology and afterward laughed at it. He also became surveyor-general.

William Mauridge, joiner, but a most exquisite mechanic, and a solid, sensible man.

Hugh Meredith, Stephen Potts, and George Webb I have characterized before.

Robert Grace, a young gentleman of some fortune, generous, lively, and witty; a lover of punning and of his friends.

Lastly, William Coleman, then a merchant's clerk, about my age, who had the coolest, clearest head, the best heart, and exactest morals of almost any man I have ever met with. He became afterward a merchant of great note and one of our provincial judges. Our friendship continued without interruption to his death, upward of forty years; and the club continued almost as long and was the best school of philosophy, morality, and politics that then existed in the province, for our queries, which were read the week preceding their discussion, put us upon reading with attention on the several subjects, that we might speak more to the purpose; and here, too, we acquired better habits of conversation, everything being studied in our rules which might prevent our disgusting each other. Hence the long continuance of the club, which I shall have frequent occasion to speak further of hereafter.

But my giving this account of it here is to show something of the interest I had, every one of these exerting themselves in recommending business to us. Breintnal particularly procured us from the Quakers the printing of forty sheets of their history, the rest being done by Keimer, and upon these we worked exceedingly hard, for the price was low. It was a folio, *pro patria* size, in pica, with long primer notes. I composed a sheet a day and Meredith worked it off at press. It was often eleven at night, and sometimes later, before I had finished my distribution for the next day's work; for the little jobs sent in by our other friends now and then put us back. But so determined I was to continue doing a sheet a day of the folio that one night, when having imposed my forms I thought my day's work over, one of them by accident was broken and two pages reduced to *pi*. I immediately distributed and composed it over again before I went to bed; and this industry, visible to our neighbors, began to give us character and credit. Particularly I was told that mention being made of the new printing-office at the merchant's every-night club, the general opinion was that it must fail, there being already two printers in the place, Keimer and Bradford. But Dr. Baird (whom you and I saw many years after at his native place, St. Andrew's, in Scotland) gave a contrary opinion: "For the industry of that Franklin," said he, "is superior to anything I ever saw of the kind. I see him still at work when I go home from club, and he is at work again before his neighbors are out of bed." This struck the rest, and we soon after had offers from one of them to supply us with stationery, but as yet we did not choose to engage in shop business.

I mention this industry more particularly and the more freely, though it seems to be talking in my own praise, that those of my posterity who shall read it may know the use of that virtue when they see its effects in my favor throughout this relation.

George Webb, who had found a female friend that lent him wherewith to purchase his time of Keimer, now came to offer himself as a journeyman to us. We could not then employ him; but I foolishly let him know, as a secret, that I soon intended to begin a newspaper and might then have work for him. My hopes of success, as I told him, were founded on this: that the then only newspaper, printed by Bradford, was a paltry thing, wretchedly managed, no way entertaining, and yet was profitable to him; I therefore freely thought a good paper would scarcely fail of good encouragement. I requested Webb not to mention it, but he told it to Keimer, who immediately, to be beforehand with me, published proposals for one himself, on which Webb was to be employed. I was vexed at this, and to counteract them, not being able to commence our paper, I wrote several amusing pieces for Bradford's paper, under the title of *The Busy-Body,* which Breintnal continued some months. By this means the attention of the public was fixed on that paper, and Keimer's proposals, which we burlesqued and ridiculed, were disregarded. He began his paper, however, and before carrying it on three-quarters of a year, with at most only ninety subscribers, he offered it me for a trifle; and I, having been ready some time to go on with it, took it in hand directly, and it proved in a few years extremely profitable to me.[2]

I perceive that I am apt to speak in the singular number, though our partnership still continued; it may be that in fact the whole management of the business lay upon me. Meredith was no compositor, a poor pressman, and seldom sober. My friends lamented my connection with him, but I was to make the best of it.

Our first papers made quite a different appearance from any before in the province; a better type and better printed; but some remarks of my writing on the dispute then going on between Governor Burnet and the Massachusetts Assembly struck the principal people, occasioned the paper and the manager of it to be much talked of, and in a few weeks brought them all to be our subscribers.

Their example was followed by many, and our number went on growing continually. This was one of the first good effects of my having learned a little to scribble. Another was that the leading men, seeing a newspaper now in the hands of those who could also handle a pen, thought it convenient to oblige and encourage me. Bradford still printed the votes and laws and other public business. He had printed an address of the House to the governor in a coarse, blundering manner. We reprinted it elegantly and correctly and sent one to every member. They were sensible of the difference, it strengthened the hands of our friends in the House, and they voted us their printers for the year ensuing.

Among my friends in the House I must not forget Mr. Hamilton, before mentioned, who was then returned from

England and had a seat in it. He interested himself for me strongly in that instance, as he did in many others afterward, continuing his patronage till his death.

Mr. Vernon about this time put me in mind of the debt I owed him, but did not press me. I wrote to him an ingenuous letter of acknowledgment, craving his forbearance a little longer, which he allowed me. As soon as I was able I paid the principal, with the interest and many thanks, so that *erratum* was in some degree corrected.

But now another difficulty came upon me, which I had never the least reason to expect. Mr. Meredith's father, who was to have paid for our printing-house, according to the expectations given me, was able to advance only one hundred pounds currency, which had been paid, and a hundred more were due to the merchant, who grew impatient and sued us all. We gave bail, but saw that if the money could not be raised in time the suit must soon come to a judgment and execution, and our hopeful prospects must with us be ruined, as the press and letters must be sold for payment, perhaps at half-price.

In this distress two true friends, whose kindness I have never forgotten nor ever shall forget while I can remember anything, came to me separately, unknown to each other, and, without any application from me, offered each of them to advance me all the money that should be necessary to enable me to take the whole business upon myself, if that should be practicable; but they did not like my continuing the partnership with Meredith, who, as they said, was often seen drunk in the street, playing at low games in ale-houses, much to our discredit. These two friends were William Coleman and Robert Grace. I told them I could not propose a separation while any prospect remained of the Merediths fulfilling their part of our agreement, because I thought myself under great obligations to them for what they had done and would do if they could, but if they finally failed in their performance and our partnership must be dissolved, I should then think myself at liberty to accept the assistance of my friends.

Thus the matter rested for some time, when I said to my partner: "Perhaps your father is dissatisfied at the part you have undertaken in this affair of ours and is unwilling to advance for you and me what he would for you. If that is the case tell me, and I will resign the whole to you and go about my business." "No," said he, "my father has really been disappointed and is really unable, and I am unwilling to distress him further. I see this is a business I am not fit for. I was bred a farmer, and it was folly in me to come to town and put myself, at thirty years of age, an apprentice to learn a new trade. Many of our Welsh people are going to settle in North Carolina, where land is cheap. I am inclined to go with them and follow my old employment; you may find friends to assist you. If you take the debts of the company upon you, return to my father the hundred pounds he has advanced, pay my little personal debts, and give me thirty pounds and a new saddle, I will relinquish the partnership and leave the whole in your hands." I agreed to this proposal; it was drawn up in writing, signed and sealed immediately. I gave him what he demanded and he went soon after to Carolina, whence he sent me next year two long letters, containing the best account that had been given of that country, the climate, the soil, and husbandry, for in those matters he was very judicious. I printed them in the paper, and they gave great satisfaction to the public.

As soon as he was gone I recurred to my two friends, and, because I would not give an unkind preference to either, I took half of what each had offered and I wanted of one, and half of the other, paid off the company's debt, and went on with the business in my own name, advertising that the partnership was dissolved. I think this was in or about the year 1729.[3]

About this time there was a cry among the people for more paper money, only fifteen thousand pounds being extant in the province, and that soon to be sunk. The wealthy inhabitants opposed any addition, being against all paper currency, from the apprehension that it would depreciate as it had done in New England, to the injury of all creditors. We had discussed this point in our Junto, where I was on the side of an addition, being persuaded that the first small sum, struck in 1723, had done much good by increasing the trade, employment and number of inhabitants in the province, since I now saw all the old houses inhabited and many new ones building; whereas I remembered well, when I first walked about the streets of Philadelphia eating my roll, I saw many of the houses in Walnut Street, between Second and Front Streets, with bills on their doors, *"To be let"* and many likewise in Chestnut Street and other streets, which made me think the inhabitants of the city were, one after another, deserting it.

Our debates possessed me so fully of the subject that I wrote and printed an anonymous pamphlet on it, entitled "The Nature and Necessity of a Paper Currency."[4] It was well received by the common people in general, but the rich men disliked it, for it increased and strengthened the clamor for more money; and they happening to have no writers among them that were able to answer it, their opposition slackened and the point was carried by a majority in the House. My friends there, who considered I had been of some service, thought fit to reward me by employing me in printing the money; a very profitable job and a great help to me. This was another advantage gained by my being able to write.

The utility of this currency became by time and experience so evident that the principles upon which it was founded were never afterward much disputed, so that it grew soon to fifty-five thousand pounds, and in 1739 to eighty thousand pounds; trade, building, and inhabitants all the while increasing. Though I now think there are limits beyond which the quantity may be hurtful.

I soon after obtained, through my friend Hamilton, the printing of the Newcastle paper money, another profitable job, as I then thought it; small things appearing great to those in small circumstances, and these to me were really great advantages, as they were great encouragements. Mr. Hamilton procured for me also the printing of the laws and votes of that government, which continued in my hands as long as I followed the business.

I now opened a small stationer's shop. I had in it blanks of all kinds, the correctest that ever appeared among us. I was assisted in that way by my friend Breintnal. I had also paper, parchment, chap-men's books, etc. One Whitemarsh, a compositor I had known in London, an excellent workman, now came to me and worked with me constantly and diligently; and I took an apprentice, the son of Aquila Rose.

I began now gradually to pay off the debt I was under for the printing-house. In order to secure my credit and character as a tradesman, I took care not only to be in *reality* industrious and frugal, but to avoid the appearances to the contrary. I dressed plain and was seen at no places of idle diversion. I never went out a-fishing or shooting; a book indeed sometimes debauched me from my work, but that was seldom, was private, and gave no scandal; and to show that I was not above my business, I sometimes brought home the paper I purchased at the stores through the streets on a wheelbarrow. Thus being esteemed an industrious, thriving young man and paying duly for what I bought, the merchants who imported stationery solicited my custom, others proposed supplying me with books, and I went on prosperously. In the mean time Keimer's credit and business declining daily, he was at last forced to sell his printing-house, to satisfy his creditors. He went to Barbadoes and there lived some years in very poor circumstances.

His apprentice, David Harry, whom I had instructed while I worked with him, set up in his place at Philadelphia, having bought his materials. I was at first apprehensive of a powerful rival in Harry, as his friends were very able and had a good deal of interest. I therefore proposed a partnership to him, which he fortunately for me rejected with scorn. He was very proud, dressed like a gentleman, lived expensively, took much diversion and pleasure abroad, ran in debt, and neglected his business; upon which all business left him, and finding nothing to do, he followed Keimer to Barbadoes, taking the printing-house with him. There this apprentice employed his former master as a journeyman; they quarreled often, and Harry went continually behindhand and at length was obliged to sell his types and return to country work in Pennsylvania. The person who bought them employed Keimer to use them, but a few years after he died.

There remained now no other printer in Philadelphia but the old Bradford; but he was rich and easy, did a little in the business by straggling hands, but was not anxious about it. However, as he held the post-office, it was imagined he had better opportunities of obtaining news, his paper was thought a better distributer of advertisements than mine, and therefore had many more; which was a profitable thing to him and a disadvantage to me. For though I did, indeed, receive and send papers by the post, yet the public opinion was otherwise; for what I did send was by bribing the riders, who took them privately, Bradford being unkind enough to forbid it, which occasioned some resentment on my part; and I thought so meanly of the practice that when I afterward came into his situation I took care never to imitate it.

I had hitherto continued to board with Godfrey, who lived in a part of my house with his wife and children and had one side of the shop for his glazier's business, though he worked little, being always absorbed in his mathematics. Mrs. Godfrey projected a match for me with a relation's daughter, took opportunities of bringing us often together, till a serious courtship on my part ensued, the girl being in herself very deserving. The old folks encouraged me by continual invitations to supper and by leaving us together, till at length it was time to explain. Mrs. Godfrey managed our little treaty. I let her know that I expected as much money with their daughter as would pay off my remaining debt for the printing-house, which I believe was not then above a hundred pounds. She brought me word they had no such sum to spare. I said they might mortgage their house in the loan office. The answer to this, after some days, was that they did not approve the match; that on inquiry of Bradford they had been informed the printing business was not a profitable one, the types would soon be worn out and more wanted; that Keimer and David Harry had failed one after the other, and I should probably soon follow them; and therefore I was forbidden the house and the daughter was shut up.

Whether this was a real change of sentiment or only artifice, on a supposition of our being too far engaged in affection to retract, and therefore that we should steal a marriage, which would leave them at liberty to give or withhold what they pleased, I know not. But I suspected the motive, resented it, and went no more. Mrs. Godfrey brought me afterward some more favorable accounts of their disposition and would have drawn me on again, but I declared absolutely my resolution to have nothing more to do with that family. This was resented by the Godfreys, we differed, and they removed, leaving me the whole house, and I resolved to take no more inmates.

But this affair having turned my thoughts to marriage, I looked round me and made overtures of acquaintance in other places, but soon found that the business of a printer being generally thought a poor one, I was not to expect money with a wife, unless with such a one as I should not otherwise think agreeable. In the mean time, that hard-to-be-governed passion of youth had hurried me frequently into intrigues with low women that fell in my way, which were attended with some expense and great inconvenience, besides a continual risk to my health by a distemper, which of all things I dreaded, though by great good luck I escaped it.

A friendly correspondence as neighbors had continued between me and Miss Read's family, who all had a regard for me from the time of my first lodging in their house. I was often invited there and consulted in their affairs, wherein I sometimes was of service. I pitied poor Miss Read's unfortunate situation, who was generally dejected, seldom cheerful, and avoided company. I considered my giddiness and inconstancy when in London as, in a great degree, the cause of her unhappiness, though the mother was good enough to think the fault more her own than mine, as she had prevented our marrying before I went thither and persuaded the other match in my absence. Our mutual affection was revived, but there were now great objections to our union. That match was indeed looked upon as invalid, a preceding wife being said to be living in England, but this could not easily be proved, because of the distance, etc.; and though there was a report of his death, it was not certain. Then, though it should be true, he had left many debts, which his successor might be called upon to pay. We ventured, however, over all these difficulties, and I took her to wife September 1st, 1730. None of the inconveniences happened that we had apprehended. She proved a good and faithful helpmate, assisted me much by attending to the shop; we throve together and ever mutually endeavored to make each other happy. Thus I corrected that great *erratum* as well as I could.

About this time our club meeting, not at a tavern, but in a little room of Mr. Grace's set apart for that purpose, a proposition was made by me that since our books were often referred to in our disquisitions upon the queries, it might be convenient to us to have them all together where we met, that upon occasion they might be consulted; and by thus clubbing our books in a common library we should, while we liked to keep them together, have each of us the advantage of using the books of all the other members, which would be nearly as beneficial as if each owned the whole. It was liked and agreed to, and we filled one end of the room with such books as we could best spare. The number was not so great as we expected, and though they had been of great use, yet some inconveniences occurring for want of due care of them, the collection, after about a year, was separated, and each took his books home again.

And now I set on foot my first project of a public nature—that for a subscription library. I drew up the proposals, got them put into form by our great scrivener, Brockden, and by the help of my friends in the Junto procured fifty subscribers of forty shillings each to begin with and ten shillings a year for fifty years, the term our company was to continue. We afterward obtained a charter, the company being increased to one hundred. This was the mother of all the North American subscription libraries, now so numerous; it is become a great thing itself and continually goes on increasing. The libraries have improved the general conversation of the Americans, made the common tradesmen and farmers as intelligent as most gentlemen from other countries, and perhaps have contributed in some degree to the stand so generally made throughout the colonies in defense of their privileges.

CHAPTER VI[1]

AT the time I established myself in Pennsylvania there was not a good bookseller's shop in any of the colonies to the southward of Boston. In New York and Philadelphia the printers were indeed stationers, but they sold only paper, almanacs, ballads, and a few common school-books. Those who loved reading were obliged to send for their books from England; the members of the Junto had each a few. We had left the ale-house where we first met and hired a room to hold our club in. I proposed that we should all of us bring our books to that room, where they would not only be ready to consult in our conferences, but become a common benefit, each of us being at liberty to borrow such as he wished to read at home. This was accordingly done and for some time contented us.

Finding the advantage of this little collection, I proposed to render the benefit from the books more common by commencing a public subscription library. I drew a sketch of the plan and rules that would be necessary, and got a skillful conveyancer, Mr. Charles Brockden, to put the whole in form of articles of agreement to be subscribed, by which each subscriber engaged to pay a certain sum down for the first purchase of the books and an annual contribution for increasing them. So few were the readers at that time in Philadelphia, and the majority of us so poor, that I was not able, with great industry, to find more than fifty persons, mostly young tradesmen, willing to pay down for this purpose forty shillings each and ten shillings per annum. With this little fund we began. The books were imported. The library was opened one day in the week for lending them to subscribers, on their promissory notes to pay double the value if not duly returned. The institution soon manifested its utility, was imitated by other towns and in other provinces. The libraries were augmented by donations, reading became fashionable, and our people, having no public amusements to divert their attention from study, became better acquainted with books, and in a few years were observed by strangers to be better instructed and more intelligent than people in the same rank generally are in other countries.

When we were about to sign the above-mentioned articles, which were to be binding on us, our heirs, etc., for fifty years, Mr. Brockden, the scrivener, said to us: "You are young men, but it is scarcely possible that any of you will live to see the expiration of the term fixed in the instrument." A number of us, however, are yet living; but the instrument was after a few years rendered null by a charter that incorporated and gave perpetuity to the company.

The objections and reluctances I met with in soliciting the subscriptions made me soon feel the impropriety of presenting one's self as the proposer of any useful project that might be supposed to raise one's reputation in the smallest degree above that of one's neighbors, when one has need of their assistance to accomplish that project. I therefore put myself as much as I could out of sight, and stated it to be a scheme of *a number of friends* who had requested me to go about and propose it to such as they thought lovers of reading. In this way my affair went on more smoothly, and I ever after practiced it on such occasions; and from my frequent successes can heartily recommend it. The present little sacrifice of your vanity will afterward be amply repaid. If it remains awhile uncertain to whom the merit belongs, some one more vain than yourself may be encouraged to claim it, and then even envy will be disposed to do you justice by plucking those assumed feathers and restoring them to their right owner.

This library afforded me the means of improvement by constant study, for which I set apart an hour or two each day, and thus repaired in some degree the loss of the learned education my father once intended for me. Reading was the only amusement I allowed myself. I spent no time in taverns, games, or frolics of any kind; and my industry in my business continued as indefatigable as it was necessary. I was indebted for my printing-house, I had a young family coming on to be educated, and I had two competitors to contend with for business who were established in the place before me. My circumstances, however, grew daily easier. My original habits of frugality continuing, and my father having, among his instructions to me when a boy, frequently repeated a proverb of Solomon, *"Seest thou a man diligent in his calling, he shall stand before kings, he shall not stand before mean men,"* I thence considered industry as a means of obtaining wealth and distinction which encouraged me—though I did not think that I should ever literally *stand before kings,* which, however, has since happened; for I have stood before *five,* and even had the honor of sitting down with one, the King of Denmark, to dinner.

We have an English proverb that says, "He that would thrive must ask his wife." It was lucky for me that I had one as much disposed to industry and frugality as myself. She assisted me cheerfully in my business, folding and stitching pamphlets, tending shop, purchasing old linen rags for the paper-makers, etc. We kept no idle servants, our table was plain and simple, our furniture of the cheapest. For instance, my breakfast for a long time was bread and milk (no tea), and I eat it out of a twopenny earthen porringer with a pewter spoon. But mark how luxuries will enter families and make a progress in spite of principle: being called one morning to breakfast, I found it in a china bowl with a spoon of silver! They had been bought for me without my knowledge by my wife, and had cost her the enormous sum of twenty-three shillings, for which she had no other excuse or apology to make but that she thought *her* husband deserved a silver spoon and china bowl as well as any of his neighbors. This was the first appearance of plate and china in our house, which afterward, in a course of years as our wealth increased, augmented gradually to several hundred pounds in value.

I had been religiously educated as a Presbyterian; but though some of the dogmas of that persuasion, such as *the eternal decrees of God, election, reprobation, etc.,* appeared to me very unintelligible, others doubtful, and I early absented myself from the public assemblies of the sect, Sunday being my studying day, I never was without some religious principles. I never doubted, for instance, the existence of a Deity—that he made the world and governed it by his providence—that the most acceptable service of God was the doing good to man—that our souls are immortal—and that all crimes will be punished and virtue rewarded, either here or hereafter. These I esteemed the essentials of every religion; and being to be found in all the religions we had in our country, I respected them all, though with different degrees of respect, as I found them more or less mixed with other articles which, without any tendency to inspire, promote, or confirm morality, served principally to divide us and make us unfriendly to one another. This respect to all, with an opinion that the worst had some good effects, induced me to avoid all discourse that might tend to lessen the good opinion another might have of his own religion; and as our province increased in people, and new places of worship were continually wanted and generally erected by voluntary contribution, my mite for such purpose, whatever might be the sect, was never refused.

Though I seldom attended any public worship, I had still an opinion of its propriety and of its utility when rightly conducted, and I regularly paid my annual subscription for the support of the only Presbyterian minister or meeting we had in Philadelphia. He used to visit me sometimes as a friend and admonish me to attend his administrations, and I was now and then prevailed on to do so, once for five Sundays successively. Had he been in my opinion a good preacher, perhaps I might have continued, notwithstanding the occasion I had for Sunday's leisure in my course of study; but his discourses were chiefly either polemic arguments or explications of the peculiar doctrines of our sect, and were all to me very dry, uninteresting, and unedifying; since not a single moral principle was inculcated or enforced, their aim seeming to be rather to make us *Presbyterians* than *good citizens.*

At length he took for his text that verse of the fourth chapter to the Philippians: *"Finally, brethren, whatsoever things are true, honest, just, pure, lovely, or of good report, if there be any virtue, or any praise, think on these things."* And I imagined in a sermon on such a text, we could not miss of having some morality. But he confined himself to five points only, as meant by the apostle: 1. Keeping holy the Sabbath day. 2. Being diligent in reading the holy Scriptures. 3. Attending duly the public worship. 4. Partaking of the Sacrament. 5. Paying due respect to God's ministers. These might be all good things; but as they were not the kind of good things that I expected from that text, I despaired of ever meeting with them from any other, was disgusted, and attended his preaching no more. I had some years before composed a little liturgy or form of prayer for my own private use (in 1728), entitled *Articles of Belief and Acts of Religion.* I returned to the use of this and went no more to the public assemblies. My conduct might be blamable, but I leave it without attempting further to excuse it; my present purpose being to relate facts and not to make apologies for them.

It was about this time I conceived the bold and arduous project of arriving at *moral perfection.* I wished to live without committing any fault at any time, and to conquer all that either natural inclination, custom, or company might lead me into. As I knew, or thought I knew, what was right and wrong, I did not see why I might not *always* do the one and avoid the other. But I soon found I had undertaken a task of more difficulty than I had imagined. While my attention was taken up and care employed in guarding against one fault, I was often surprised by another; habit took the advantage of inattention; inclination was sometimes too strong for reason. I concluded at length that the mere speculative conviction that it was our interest to be completely virtuous was not sufficient to prevent our slipping, and that the contrary habits must be broken and good ones acquired and established before we can have any dependence on a steady, uniform rectitude of conduct. For this purpose I therefore tried the following method.

In the various enumerations of the *moral virtues* I had met with in my reading, I found the catalogue more or less numerous, as different writers included more or fewer ideas under the same name. *Temperance,* for example, was by some confined to eating and drinking; while by others it was extended to mean the moderating every other pleasure, appetite, inclination, or passion, bodily or mentally, even to our avarice and ambition. I proposed to myself, for the sake of clearness, to use rather more names, with fewer ideas annexed to each, than a few names with more ideas; and I included under thirteen names of virtues all that at that time occurred to me as necessary or desirable, and annexed to each a short precept which fully expressed the extent I gave to its meaning.

The names of *virtues,* with their precepts, were:

1. TEMPERANCE. — Eat not to dullness; drink not to elevation.

2. SILENCE. — Speak not but what may benefit others or yourself; avoid trifling conversation.

3. ORDER. — Let all your things have their places; let each part of your business have its time.

4. RESOLUTION. — Resolve to perform what you ought; perform without fail what you resolve.

5. FRUGALITY. — Make no expense but to do good to others or yourself; that is, waste nothing.

6. INDUSTRY. — Lose no time; be always employed in something useful; cut off all unnecessary actions.

7. SINCERITY. — Use no hurtful deceit; think innocently and justly; and, if you speak, speak accordingly.

8. JUSTICE. — Wrong none by doing injuries or omitting the benefits that are your duty.

9. MODERATION. — Avoid extremes; forbear resenting injuries, so much as you think they deserve.

10. CLEANLINESS. — Tolerate no uncleanliness in body, clothes, or habitation.

11. TRANQUILLITY.—Be not disturbed at trifles or at accidents common or unavoidable.

12. CHASTITY. . . . .

13. HUMILITY.—Imitate Jesus and Socrates.

My intention being to acquire the habitude of all these virtues, I judged it would be well not to distract my attention by attempting the whole at once, but to fix it on *one* of them at a time; and when I should be master of that, then to proceed to another; and so on till I should have gone through the thirteen. And as the previous acquisition of some might facilitate the acquisition of certain others, I arranged them with the view as they stand above. *Temperance* first, as it tends to procure that coolness and clearness of head which is so necessary where constant vigilance was to be kept up and a guard maintained against the unremitting attraction of ancient habits and the force of perpetual temptations. This being acquired and established, *silence* would be more easy; and my desire being to gain knowledge at the same time that I improved in virtue, and considering that in conversation it was obtained rather by the use of the ear than of the tongue, and therefore wishing to break a habit I was getting into of prattling, punning, and jesting, which only made me acceptable to trifling company, I gave *silence* the second place. This and the next, *order,* I expected would allow me more time for attending to my project and my studies. *Resolution,* once become habitual, would keep me firm in my endeavors to obtain all the subsequent virtues; *frugality* and *industry* relieving me from my remaining debt, and producing affluence and independence, would make more easy the practice of *sincerity* and *justice,* etc., etc. Conceiving, then, that, agreeably to the advice of Pythagoras in his *Golden Verses,* daily examination would be necessary, I contrived the following method for conducting that examination.

I made a little book, in which I allotted a page for each of the virtues. I ruled each page with red ink, so as to have seven columns, one for each day of the week, marking each column with a letter for the day. I crossed these columns with thirteen red lines, marking the beginning of each line with the first letter of one of the virtues; on which line, and in its proper column, I might mark, by a little black spot, every fault I found upon examination to have been committed respecting that virtue upon that day.[2]

I determined to give a week's strict attention to each of the virtues successively. Thus in the first week my great guard was to avoid every day the least offense against *temperance;* leaving other virtues to their ordinary chance, only marking every evening the faults of the day. Thus if in the first week I could keep my first line, marked Tem. clear of spots, I supposed the habit of that virtue so much strengthened and its opposite weakness that I might venture extending my attention to include the next, and for the following week keep both lines clear of spots. Proceeding thus to the last,

FORM OF THE PAGES.
TEMPERANCE.

Eat not to dullness; drink not to elevation.

	Sun	M.	T.	W.	Th.	F.	S.
Tem.							
Sil.	*	*		*		*	
Ord.	*	*			*	*	*
Res.		*				*	
Fru.		*				*	
Ind.			*				
Sinc.							
Jus.							
Mod.							
Clea.							
Tran.							
Chas.							
Hum.							

I could get through a course complete in thirteen weeks and four courses in a year. And like him who, having a garden to weed, does not attempt to eradicate all the bad herbs at once, which would exceed his reach and his strength, but works on one of the beds at a time, and having accomplished the first proceeds to the second, so I should have, I hoped, the encouraging pleasure of seeing on my pages the progress made in virtue, by clearing successively my lines of their spots; till in the end, by a number of courses, I should be happy in viewing a clean book after a thirteen weeks' daily examination.

This my little book had for its motto these lines from Addison's *Cato:*

"Here will I hold. If there's a power above us
(And that there is, all nature cries aloud
Through all her works), He must delight in virtue;
And that which He delights in must be happy."

Another from Cicero:

"O vitæ Philosophia dux! O virtutum indagatrix expultrixque vitiorum! Unus dies, bene et ex præceptis tuis actus, peccanti immortalitati est anteponcndus."

Another from the Proverbs of Solomon, speaking of wisdom or virtue:

"Length of days is in her right hand, and in her left hand riches and honor. Her ways are ways of pleasantness, and all her paths are peace."

And conceiving God to be the fountain of wisdom, I thought it right and necessary to solicit his assistance for obtaining it; to this end I formed the following little prayer, which was prefixed to my tables of examination for daily use:

"O powerful Goodness! bountiful Father! merciful Guide! Increase in me that wisdom which discovers my truest interest. Strengthen my resolution to perform what that wisdom dictates. Accept my kind offices to Thy other children as the only return in my power for Thy continual favors to me."

I used also sometimes a little prayer which I took from Thomson's *Poems,* viz:

"Father of light and life, thou Good Supreme!
O teach me what is good; teach me Thyself!
Save me from folly, vanity, and vice,
From every low pursuit; and feed my soul
With knowledge, conscious peace, and virtue pure;
Sacred, substantial, never-fading bliss!"

The precept of *order* requiring that *every part of my business should have its allotted time,* one page in my little book contained the appended scheme of employment for the twenty-four hours of a natural day.

I entered upon the execution of this plan for self examination and continued it with occasional intermissions for some time. I was surprised to find myself so much fuller of faults than I had imagined; but I had the satisfaction of seeing them diminish. To avoid the trouble of renewing now and then my little book, which, by scraping out the marks on the paper of old faults to make room for new ones in a new course, became full of holes, I transferred my tables and precepts to the ivory leaves of a memorandum book, on which the lines were drawn with red ink, that made a durable stain; and on those lines I marked my faults with a black-lead pencil, which marks I could easily wipe out with a wet sponge. After awhile I went through one course only in a year, and afterward only one in several years, till at length I omitted them entirely, being employed in voyages and business abroad with a multiplicity of affairs that interfered; but I always carried my little book with me.

SCHEME
Hours.

MORNING. The *Question. What* good shall I do this day?	5 6 7	Rise, wash, and address *Powerful Goodness!* Contrive day's business and take the resolution of the day; prosecute the present study and breakfast.
	8 9 10 11	Work.
NOON.	12 1	Read or look over my accounts and dine.
AFTERNOON.	2 3 4 5	Work.
EVENING. The *Question.* What good have I done to-day?	6 7 8 9	Put things in their places. Supper. Music or diversion or conversation. Examination of the day.
NIGHT.	10 11 12 1 2 3 4	Sleep.

My scheme of *order* gave me the most trouble, and I found that though it might be practicable where a man's business was such as to leave him the disposition of his time, that of a journeyman printer, for instance, it was not possible to be exactly observed by a

81

master who must mix with the world and often receive people of business at their own hours. Order, too, with regard to places for things, papers, etc., I found extremely difficult to acquire. I had not been early accustomed to *method,* and having an exceedingly good memory, I was not so sensible of the inconvenience attending want of method. This article, therefore, cost me much painful attention, and my faults in it vexed me so much, and I made so little progress in amendment and had such frequent relapses, that I was almost ready to give up the attempt and content myself with a faulty character in that respect. Like the man who, in buying an ax of a smith, my neighbor, desired to have the whole of its surface as bright as the edge. The smith consented to grind it bright for him if he would turn the wheel; he turned, while the smith pressed the broad face of the ax hard and heavily on the stone, which made the turning of it very fatiguing. The man came every now and then from the wheel to see how the work went on; and at length would take his ax as it was, without further grinding. "No," said the smith, "turn on, turn on, we shall have it bright by and by; as yet it is only speckled." "Yes," said the man, "but *I think I like a speckled ax best!*" And I believe this may have been the case with many who, having for want of some such means as I employed found the difficulty of obtaining good and breaking bad habits in other points of vice and virtue, have given up the struggle and concluded that *"a speckled ax is best."* For something, that pretended to be reason, was every now and then suggesting to me that such extreme nicety as I exacted of myself might be a kind of foppery in morals which, if it were known, would make me ridiculous; that a perfect character might be attended with the inconvenience of being envied and hated; and that a benevolent man should allow a few faults in himself to keep his friends in countenance.

In truth, I found myself incorrigible with respect to *order;* and now I am grown old and my memory bad, I feel very sensibly the want of it. But on the whole, though I never arrived at the perfection I had been so ambitious of obtaining, but fell far short of it, yet I was, by the endeavor, a better and a happier man than I otherwise should have been if I had not attempted it; as those who aim at perfect writing by imitating the engraved copies, though they never reach the wished-for excellence of those copies, their hand is mended by the endeavor and is tolerable while it continues fair and legible.

It may be well my posterity should be informed that to this little artifice, with the blessing of God, their ancestor owed the constant felicity of his life down to his seventy-ninth year, in which this is written. What reverses may attend the remainder is in the hand of Providence; but if they arrive, the reflection on past happiness enjoyed ought to help his bearing them with more resignation. To *temperance* he ascribes his long-continued health and what is still left to him of a good constitution; to *industry* and *frugality* the early easiness of his circumstances and acquisition of his fortune, with all that knowledge that enabled him to be a useful citizen and obtained for him some degree of reputation among the learned; to *sincerity* and *justice* the confidence of his country and the honorable employs it conferred upon him; and to the joint influence of the whole mass of the virtues, even in the imperfect state he was able to acquire them, all that evenness of temper and that cheerfulness in conversation which makes his company still sought for and agreeable even to his young acquaintance. I hope, therefore, that some of my descendants may follow the example and reap the benefit.

It will be remarked that though my scheme was not wholly without religion, there was in it no mark of any of the distinguishing tenets of any particular sect. I had purposely avoided them; for being fully persuaded of the utility and excellency of my method, and that it might be serviceable to people in all religions, and intending some time or other to publish it, I would not have anything in it that should prejudice any one, of any sect, against it. I proposed writing a little comment on each virtue, in which I would have shown the advantages of possessing it and the mischiefs attending its opposite vice. I should have called my book *The Art of Virtue,* because it would have shown the means and manner of obtaining virtue, which would have distinguished it from the mere exhortation to be good that does not instruct and indicate the means; but is like the apostle's man of verbal charity, who, without showing to the naked and hungry how or where they might get clothes or victuals, only exhorted them to be fed and clothed (James, ii., 15, 16).

But it so happened that my intention of writing and publishing this comment was never fulfilled. I had, indeed, from time to time put down short hints of the sentiments and reasonings to be made use of in it, some of which I have still by me; but the necessary close attention to private business in the earlier part of life and public business since have occasioned my postponing it. For, it being connected in my mind with *a great and extensive project* that required the whole man to execute and which an unforeseen succession of employs prevented my attending to, it has hitherto remained unfinished.

In this piece it was my design to explain and enforce this doctrine, *that vicious actions are not hurtful because they are forbidden, but forbidden because they are hurtful,* the nature of man alone considered; that it was, therefore, every one's interest to be virtuous who wished to be happy even in this world; and I should from this circumstance (there being always in the world a number of rich merchants, nobility, states, and princes who have need of honest instruments for the management of their affairs, and such being so rare) have endeavored to convince young persons that no qualities are so likely to make a poor man's fortune as those of *probity* and *integrity.*

My list of virtues contained at first but twelve; but a Quaker friend having kindly informed me that I was generally thought proud, that my pride showed itself frequently in conversation, that I was not content with being in the right when discussing any point, but was overbearing and rather insolent, of which he convinced me by mentioning several instances, I determined to endeavor to cure myself, if I could, of this vice or folly among the rest; and I added *humility* to my list, giving an extensive meaning to the word.

I cannot boast of much success in acquiring the *reality* of this virtue, but I had a good deal with regard to the appearance of it. I made it a rule to forbear all direct contradiction to the sentiments of others and all positive assertion of my own. I even forbid myself, agreeably to the old laws of our Junto, the use of every word or expression in the language that imported a fixed opinion; such as *certainly, undoubtedly,* etc., and I adopted instead of them, *I conceive, I comprehend,* or *I imagine,* a thing to be so or so; or it so *appears to me at present.* When another asserted something that I thought an error, I denied myself the pleasure of contradicting him abruptly and of showing immediately some absurdity in his proposition; and in answering I began by observing that in certain cases or circumstances his opinion would be right, but in the present case there *appeared* or *seemed to me* some difference, etc. I soon found the advantage of this change in my manners; the conversations I engaged in went on more pleasantly. The modest way in which I proposed my opinions procured them a readier reception and less contradiction; I had less mortification when I was found to be in the wrong; and I more easily prevailed with others to give up their mistakes and join with me when I happened to be in the right.

And this mode, which I at first put on with some violence to natural inclination, became at length easy and so habitual to me that perhaps for the last fifty years no one has ever heard a dogmatical expression escape me. And to this habit (after my character of integrity) I think it principally owing that I had early so much weight with my fellow-citizens when I proposed new institutions or alterations in the old; and so much influence in public councils when I became a member; for I was but a bad speaker, never eloquent, subject to much hesitation in my choice of words, hardly correct in language, and yet I generally carried my point.

In reality there is, perhaps, no one of our natural passions so hard to subdue as pride. Disguise it, struggle with it, stifle it, mortify it as much as one pleases, it is still alive and will every now and then peep out and show itself; you will see it, perhaps, often in this history. For even if I could conceive that I had completely overcome it, I should probably be *proud* of my *humility.*

CHAPTER VII

HAVING mentioned a *great and extensive project* which I had conceived, it seems proper that some account should be here given of that project and its object. Its first rise in my mind appears in the following little paper, accidentally preserved, viz.:

"Observations on my reading history in the library,
May 9th, 1731.

"That the great affairs of the world, the wars and revolutions, are carried on and effected by parties.

"That the view of these parties is their present general interest, or what they take to be such.

"That the different views of these different parties occasion all confusion.

"That while a party is carrying on a general design, each man has his particular private interest in view.

"That as soon as a party has gained its general point, each member becomes intent upon his particular interest; which thwarting others, breaks that party into divisions and occasions more confusion.

"That few in public affairs act from a mere view of the good of their country, whatever they may pretend, and though their actings bring real good to their country, yet men primarily considered that their own and their country's interest were united, and so did not act from a principle of benevolence.

"That fewer still in public affairs act with a view to the good of mankind.

"There seems to me at present to be great occasion for raising a *united party for virtue,* by forming the virtuous and good men of all nations into a regular body, to be governed by suitable good and wise rules, which good and wise men may probably be more unanimous in their obedience to than common people are to common laws.

"I at present think that whoever attempts this aright and is well qualified cannot fail of pleasing God and of meeting with success."

Revolving this project in my mind as to be undertaken hereafter, when my circumstances should afford me the necessary leisure, I put down from time to time on pieces of paper such thoughts as occurred to me respecting it. Most of these are lost; but I find one purporting to be the substance of an intended creed, containing, as I thought, the essentials of every known religion, and being free of everything that might shock the professors of any religion. It is expressed in these words, viz.:

"That there is one God, who made all things.

"That he governs the world by his providence.

"That he ought to be worshiped by adoration, prayer, and thanksgiving.

"But that the most acceptable service to God is doing good to man.

"That the soul is immortal.

"And that God will certainly reward virtue and punish vice, either here or hereafter."

My ideas at that time were that the sect should be begun and spread at first among young and single men only; that each person to be initiated should not only declare his assent to such creed, but should have exercised himself with the thirteen weeks' examination and practice of the virtues, as in the before-mentioned model; that the existence of such a society should be kept a secret till it was become considerable, to prevent solicitations for the admission of improper persons; but that the members should, each of them, search among his acquaintance for ingenious, well-disposed youths, to whom, with prudent caution, the scheme should be gradually communicated. That the members should engage to afford their advice, assistance, and support to each other in promoting one another's interest, business, and advancement in life. That for distinction we should be called the SOCIETY OF THE FREE AND EASY. Free, as being, by the general practice and habits of the virtues, free from the dominion of vice; and particularly, by the practice of industry and frugality, free from debt, which exposes a man to constraint and a species of slavery to his creditors.

This is as much as I can now recollect of the project, except that I communicated it in part to two young men who adopted it with some enthusiasm; but my then narrow circumstances and the necessity I was under of sticking close to my business occasioned my postponing the further prosecution of it at that time, and my multifarious occupations, public and private, induced me to continue postponing, so that it has been omitted till I have no longer strength or activity left sufficient for such an enterprise. Though I am still of opinion it was a practicable scheme, and might have been very useful by forming a great number of good citizens, and I was not discouraged by the seeming magnitude of the undertaking, as I have always thought that one man of tolerable abilities may work great changes and accomplish great affairs among mankind if he first forms a good plan, and cutting off all amusements or other employments that would divert his attention, makes the execution of that same plan his sole study and business.

In 1732 I first published my almanac, under the name of Richard Saunders; it was continued by me about twenty-five years and commonly called "Poor Richard's Almanac." I endeavored to make it both entertaining and useful, and it accordingly came to be in such demand that I reaped considerable profit from it, vending annually near ten thousand. And observing that it was generally read, scarce any neighborhood in the province being without it, I considered it as a proper vehicle for conveying instruction among the common people, who bought scarcely any other books. I therefore filled all the little spaces that occurred between the remarkable days in the calendar with proverbial sentences, chiefly such as inculcated industry and frugality as the means of procuring wealth, and thereby securing virtue; it being more difficult for a man in want to act always honestly, as, to use here one of those proverbs, *it is hard for an empty sack to stand upright.*

These proverbs, which contained the wisdom of many ages and nations, I assembled and formed into a connected discourse prefixed to the almanac of 1757 as the harangue of a wise old man to the people attending an auction. The bringing all these scattered counsels thus into a focus enabled them to make greater impression. The piece, being universally approved, was copied in all the newspapers of the American continent, reprinted in Britain on a large sheet of paper to be stuck up in houses; two translations were made of it in France, and great numbers bought by the clergy and gentry to distribute gratis among their poor parishioners and tenants. In Pennsylvania, as it discouraged useless expense in foreign superfluities, some thought it had its share of influence in producing that growing plenty of money which was observable for several years after its publication.

I considered my newspaper also as another means of communicating instruction, and in that view frequently reprinted in it extracts from the *Spectator* and other moral writers, and sometimes published little pieces of my own, which had been first composed for reading in our Junto. Of these are a Socratic dialogue tending to prove that whatever might be his parts and abilities, a vicious man could not properly be called a man of sense; and a discourse on self-denial, showing that virtue was not secure till its practice became a *habitude* and was free from the opposition of contrary inclinations. These may be found in the papers about the beginning of 1735.

In the conduct of my newspaper I carefully excluded all libeling and personal abuse, which is of late years become so disgraceful to our country. Whenever I was solicited to insert anything of that kind and the writers pleaded, as they generally did, the liberty of the press—and that a newspaper was like a stagecoach, in which any one who would pay had a right to a place—my answer was that

I would print the piece separately if desired, and the author might have as many copies as he pleased to distribute himself, but that I would not take upon me to spread his detraction, and that having contracted with my subscribers to furnish them with what might be either useful or entertaining, I could not fill their papers with private altercation, in which they had no concern, without doing them manifest injustice. Now many of our printers make no scruple of gratifying the malice of individuals by false accusations of the fairest characters among ourselves, augmenting animosity even to the producing of duels; and are, moreover, so indiscreet as to print scurrilous reflections on the government of neighboring States, and even on the conduct of our best national allies, which may be attended with the most pernicious consequences. These things I mention as a caution to young printers, and that they may be encouraged not to pollute their presses and disgrace their profession by such infamous practices, but refuse steadily; as they may see by my example that such a course of conduct will not on the whole be injurious to their interests.

In 1733 I sent one of my journeymen to Charleston, South Carolina, where a printer was wanting. I furnished him with a press and letters on an agreement of partnership, by which I was to receive one-third of the profits of the business, paying one-third of the expense. He was a man of learning, but ignorant in matters of account; and though he sometimes made me remittances, I could get no account from him, nor any satisfactory state of our partnership while he lived. On his decease the business was continued by his widow, who, being born and bred in Holland, where, as I have been informed, the knowledge of accounts makes a part of female education, she not only sent me as clear a statement as she could find of the transactions past, but continued to account with the greatest regularity and exactness every quarter afterward, and managed the business with such success that she not only reputably brought up a family of children, but at the expiration of the term was able to purchase of me the printing-house and establish her son in it.

I mention this affair chiefly for the sake of recommending that branch of education for our young women as likely to be of more use to them and their children, in case of widowhood, than either music or dancing; by preserving them from losses by imposition of crafty men and enabling them to continue, perhaps, a profitable mercantile house, with established correspondence, till a son is grown up fit to undertake and go on with it, to the lasting advantage and enriching of the family.

About the year 1734 there arrived among us a young Presbyterian preacher, named Hemphill, who delivered with a good voice, and apparently extempore, most excellent discourses, which drew together considerable numbers of different persuasions, who joined in admiring them. Among the rest I became one of his constant hearers, his sermons pleasing me, as they had little of the dogmatical kind, but inculcated strongly the practice of virtue, or what in the religious style are called *good works*. Those, however, of our congregation who considered themselves as orthodox Presbyterians disapproved his doctrine, and were joined by most of the old ministers, who arraigned him of heterodoxy before the synod, in order to have him silenced. I became his zealous partisan, and contributed all I could to raise a party in his favor and combated for him awhile with some hopes of success. There was much scribbling *pro* and *con* upon the occasion, and finding that though an elegant preacher he was but a poor writer, I wrote for him two or three pamphlets and a piece in the *Gazette* of April 1735. Those pamphlets, as is generally the case with controversial writings, though eagerly read at the time, were soon out of vogue, and I question whether a single copy of them now exists.

During the contest an unlucky occurrence hurt his cause exceedingly. One of our adversaries having heard him preach a sermon that was much admired, thought he had somewhere read the sermon before, or at least a part of it. On searching, he found that part quoted at length in one of the British reviews from a discourse of Dr. Foster's. This defection gave many of our party disgust, who accordingly abandoned his cause and occasioned our more speedy discomfiture in the synod. I stuck by him, however. I rather approved his giving us good sermons composed by others than bad ones of his own manufacture, though the latter was the practice of our common teachers. He afterward acknowledged to me that none of those he preached were his own, adding that his memory was such as enabled him to retain and repeat any sermon after once reading only. On our defeat he left us in search elsewhere of better fortune, and I quitted the congregation, never attending it after, though I continued many years my subscription for the support of its ministers.

I had begun in 1733 to study languages. I soon made myself so much a master of the French as to be able to read the books in that language with ease. I then undertook the Italian. An acquaintance who was also learning it used often to tempt me to play chess with him. Finding this took up too much of the time I had to spare for study, I at length refused to play any more, unless on this condition, that the victor in every game should have a right to impose a task, either of parts of the grammar, to be got by heart, or in translations, which tasks the vanquished was to perform upon honor before our next meeting. As we played pretty equally, we thus beat one another into that language. I afterward, with a little painstaking, acquired as much of the Spanish as to read their books also.

I have already mentioned that I had only one year's instruction in a Latin school, and that when very young, after which I neglected that language entirely. But when I had attained an acquaintance with the French, Italian, and Spanish, I was surprised to find, on looking over a Latin Testament, that I understood more of that language than I had imagined; which encouraged me to apply myself again to the study of it, and I met with more success, as those preceding languages had greatly smoothed my way.

From these circumstances I have thought there is some inconsistency in our common mode of teaching languages. We are told that it is proper to begin first with the Latin, and having acquired that it will be more easy to attain those modern languages which are derived from it; and yet we do not begin with the Greek in order more easily to acquire the Latin. It is true that if we can clamber and get to the top of a staircase without using the steps, we shall more easily gain them in descending; but certainly if we begin with the lowest we shall with more ease ascend to the top; and I would therefore offer it to the consideration of those who superintendent the education of our youth whether, since many of those who begin with the Latin quit the same after spending some years without having made any great proficiency, and what they have learned becomes almost useless, so that their time has been lost, it would not have been better to have begun with the French, proceeding to the Italian and Latin. For though after spending the same time they should quit the study of languages and never arrive at the Latin, they would, however, have acquired another tongue or two that, being in modern use, might be serviceable to them in common life.

After ten years' absence from Boston, and having become easy in my circumstances, I made a journey thither to visit my relations, which I could not sooner afford. In returning I called at Newport to see my brother James, then settled there with his printing-house. Our former differences were forgotten and our meeting was very cordial and affectionate. He was fast declining in health, and requested me that in case of his death, which he appre-hended was not far distant, I would take home his son, then but ten years of age, and bring him up to the printing business. This I, accordingly performed, sending him a few years to school before I took him into the office. His mother carried on the business till he was grown up, when I assisted him with an assortment of new types, those of his father being in a manner worn out. Thus it was that I made my brother ample amends for the service I had deprived him of by leaving him so early.

In 1736 I lost one of my sons, a fine boy of four years old, by small-pox, taken in the common way. I long regretted him bitterly and still regret that I had not given it to him by inoculation. This I mention for the sake of parents who omit that operation on the supposition that they should never forgive themselves if a child died under it, my example showing that the regret may be the same either way, and therefore that the safer should be chosen.

Our club, the Junto, was found so useful and afforded such satisfaction to the members that some were desirous of introducing their friends, which could not well be done without exceeding what we had settled as a convenient number, viz., twelve. We had from the beginning made it a rule to keep our institution a secret, which was pretty well observed; the intention was to avoid applications of improper persons for admittance, some of whom, perhaps, we might find it difficult to refuse. I was one of those who were against any addition to our number, but instead of it made in writing a proposal that every member separately should endeavor to form a subordinate club, with the same rules respecting queries, etc., and without informing them of the connection with the Junto. The advantages proposed were the improvement of so many more young citizens by the use of our institutions; our better acquaintance with the general sentiments of the inhabitants on any occasion, as the Junto member might propose what queries we should desire and was to report to the Junto what passed at his separate club; the promotion of our particular interests in business by more extensive recommendation, and the Increase of our influence in public affairs, and our power of doing good by spreading through the several clubs the sentiments of the Junto.

The project was approved, and every member undertook to form his club; but they did not all succeed. Five or six only were completed, which were called by different names, as the *Vine*, the *Union*, the *Band*. They were useful to themselves and afforded us a good deal of amusement, information, and instruction; besides answering, in some considerable degree, our views of influencing the public on particular occasions, of which I shall give instances in course of time as they happened.

My first promotion was my being chosen, in 1736, clerk of the General Assembly. The choice was made that year without opposition; but the year following, when I was again proposed (the choice, like that of the members, being annual), a new member made a long speech against me in order to favor some other candidate. I was, however, chosen, which was the more agreeable to me, as, besides the pay for the immediate service of clerk, the place gave me an opportunity of keeping up an interest among the members, which secured to me the business of printing the votes, laws, paper money, and other occasional jobs for the public that, on the whole, were very profitable.

I therefore did not like the opposition of this new member, who was a gentleman of fortune and education, with talents that were likely to give him in time great influence in the House, which indeed afterward happened. I did not, however, aim at gaining his favor by paying any servile respect to him, but after some time took this other method. Having heard that he had in his library a certain very scarce and curious book, I wrote a note to him expressing my desire of perusing that book and requesting that he would do me the favor of lending it to me for a few days. He sent it immediately; and I returned it in about a week with another note expressing strongly the sense of the favor. When we next met in the House he spoke to me, which he had never done before, and with great civility; and he ever after manifested a readiness to serve me on all occasions, so that we became great friends, and our friendship continued to his death. This is another instance of the truth of an old maxim I had learned, which says: *"He that has once done you a kindness will be more ready to do you another than he whom you yourself have obliged."* And it shows how much more profitable it is prudently to remove than to resent, return and continue inimical proceedings.

In 1737 Colonel Spotswood, late Governor of Virginia and then Postmaster-General, being dissatisfied with the conduct of his deputy at Philadelphia respecting some negligence in rendering and want of exactness in framing his accounts, took from him the commission and offered it to me. I accepted it readily and found it of great advantage; for though the salary was small, it facilitated the correspondence that improved my newspaper, increased the number demanded, as well as the advertisements to be inserted, so that it came to afford me a considerable income. My old competitor's newspaper declined proportionably, and I was satisfied without retaliating his refusal, while postmaster, to permit my papers being carried by the riders. Thus he suffered greatly from his neglect in due accounting; and I mention it as a lesson to those young men who may be employed in managing affairs for others, that they should always render accounts and make remittances with great clearness and punctuality. The character of observing such a conduct is the most powerful of all recommendations to new employments and increase of business.

I began now to turn my thoughts to public affairs, beginning, however, with small matters. The city watch was one of the first things that I conceived to want regulation. It was managed by the constables of the respective wards in turn; the constable summoned a number of housekeepers to attend him for the night. Those who chose never to attend paid him six shillings a year to be excused, which was supposed to go to hiring substitutes, but was in reality much more than was necessary for that purpose, and made the constableship a place of profit; and the constable, for a little drink, often got such ragamuffins about him as a watch that respectable housekeepers did not choose to mix with. Walking the rounds, too, was often neglected, and most of the nights spent in tippling. I thereupon wrote a paper, to be read in the Junto, representing these irregularities, but insisting more particularly on the inequality of the six-shilling tax of the constable, respecting the circumstances of those who paid it; since a poor widow housekeeper, all whose property to be guarded by the watch did not perhaps exceed the value of fifty pounds, paid as much as the wealthiest merchant, who had thousands of pounds' worth of goods in his stores.

On the whole, I proposed, as a more effectual watch, the hiring of proper men to serve constantly in the business, and as a more equitable way of supporting the charge, the levying a tax that should be proportioned to the property. This idea being approved by the Junto was communicated to the other clubs, but as originating in each of them; and though the plan was not immediately carried into execution, yet by preparing the minds of people for the change it paved the way for the law obtained a few years after, when the members of our club were grown into more influence.

About this time I wrote a paper (first to be read in the Junto, but it was afterward published) on the different accidents and carelessnesses by which houses were set on fire, with cautions against them and means proposed of avoiding them. This was spoken of as a useful piece, and gave rise to a project, which soon followed it, of forming a company for the more ready extinguishing of fires and mutual assistance in removing and securing of goods when in danger. Associates in this scheme were presently found amounting to thirty. Our articles of agreement obliged every member to keep always in good order and fit for use a certain number of leathern buckets, with strong bags and baskets (for packing and transporting of goods), which were to be brought to every fire, and we agreed, about once a month, to spend a social evening together, in discoursing and communicating such ideas as occurred to us upon the subject of fires as might be useful in our conduct on such occasions.

The utility of this institution soon appeared, and many more desiring to be admitted than we thought convenient for one company they were advised to form another, which was accordingly done, and thus went on one new company after another till they became so numerous as to include most of the inhabitants who were men of property, and now at the time of my writing this, though upward of fifty years since its establishment, that which I first formed, called the Union Fire Company, still subsists, though the first members are all deceased but one, who is older by a year than I am. The fines that have been paid by members for absence at the monthly meetings have been applied to the purchase of fire-engines, ladders, fire-hooks, and other useful implements for each company; so that I question whether there is a city in the world better provided with the means of putting a stop to beginning conflagrations, and, in fact, since these institutions the city has never lost by fire more than one or two houses at a time, and the flames have often been extinguished before the house in which they began has been half consumed.

CHAPTER VIII

IN 1739, arrived among us from Ireland the Reverend Mr. Whitefield, who had made himself remarkable there as an itinerant preacher. He was at first permitted to preach in some of our churches; but the clergy taking a dislike to him, soon refused him their pulpits, and he was obliged to preach in the fields. The multitudes of all sects and denominations that attended his sermons were enormous, and it was a matter of speculation to me, who was one of the number, to observe the extraordinary influence of his oratory on his hearers, and how much they admired and respected him, notwithstanding his common abuse of them, by assuring them they were naturally *half beasts and half devils*. It was wonderful to see the change soon made in the manners of our inhabitants. From being thoughtless or indifferent about religion, it seemed as if all the world were growing religious, so that one could not walk through the town in an evening without hearing psalms sung in different families of every street.

And it being found inconvenient to assemble in the open air, subject to its inclemencies, the building of a house to meet in was no sooner proposed, and persons appointed to receive contributions, than sufficient sums were soon received to procure the ground and erect the building, which was one hundred feet long and seventy broad; and the work was carried on with such spirit as to be finished in a much shorter time than could have been expected. Both house and ground were vested in trustees, expressly for the use of *any preacher of any religious persuasion* who might desire to say something to the people at Philadelphia, the design in building being not to accommodate any particular sect, but the inhabitants in general; so that even if the Mufti of Constantinople were to send a missionary to preach Mohammedanism to us, he would find a pulpit at his service.

Mr. Whitefield, on leaving us, went preaching all the way through the colonies to Georgia. The settlement of that province had been lately begun, but instead of being made with hardy, industrious husbandmen accustomed to labor, the only people fit for such an enterprise, it was with families of broken shopkeepers and other insolvent debtors; many of indolent and idle habits, taken out of the jails, who, being set down in the woods, unqualified for clearing land and unable to endure the hardships of a new settlement, perished in numbers, leaving many helpless children unprovided for. The sight of their miserable situation inspired the benevolent heart of Mr. Whitefield with the idea of building an orphan house there, in which they might be supported and educated. Returning northward, he preached up this charity and made large collections; for his eloquence had a wonderful power over the hearts and purses of his hearers, of which I myself was an instance.

I did not disapprove of the design, but as Georgia was then destitute of materials and workmen and it was proposed to send them from Philadelphia at a great expense, I thought it would have been better to have built the house at Philadelphia and brought the children to it. This I advised; but he was resolute in his first project, rejected my counsel, and I therefore refused to contribute. I happened soon after to attend one of his sermons, in the course of which I perceived he intended to finish with a collection, and I silently resolved that he should get nothing from me. I had in my pocket a handful of copper money, three or four silver dollars, and five pistoles in gold. As he proceeded I began to soften and concluded to give the copper. Another stroke of his oratory made me ashamed of that and determined me to give the silver; and he finished so admirably that I emptied my pocket wholly into the collector's dish, gold and all. At this sermon there was also one of our club who, being of my sentiments respecting the building in Georgia and suspecting a collection might be intended, had by precaution emptied his pockets before he came from home. Toward the conclusion of the discourse, however, he felt a strong inclination to give, and applied to a neighbor who stood near him to lend him some money for the purpose. The request was fortunately made to perhaps the only man in the company who had the firmness not to be affected by the preacher. His answer was, "At any other time, friend Hopkinson, I would lend to thee freely, but not now, for thee seems to be out of thy right senses."

Some of Mr. Whitefield's enemies affected to suppose that he would apply these collections to his own private emolument; but I, who was intimately acquainted with him, being employed in printing his sermons and journals, never had the least suspicion of his integrity, but am to this day decidedly of opinion that he was in all his conduct a perfectly *honest man;* and methinks my testimony in his favor ought to have the more weight, as we had no religious connection. He used, indeed, sometimes to pray for my conversion, but he never had the satisfaction of believing that his prayers were heard. Ours was a mere civil friendship, sincere on both sides, and lasted to his death.

The following instance will show the terms on which we stood. Upon one of his arrivals from England at Boston he wrote to me that he should come soon to Philadelphia, but knew not where he could lodge when there, as he understood his old friend and host, Mr. Benezet, was removed to Germantown. My answer was: "You know my house; if you can make shift with its scanty accommodations, you will be most heartily welcome." He replied that if I made that kind offer for *Christ's* sake I should not miss of a reward. And I returned: "Don't let me be mistaken; it was not for *Christ's* sake, but for *your* sake." One of our common acquaintance jocosely remarked that knowing it to be the custom of the saints when they received any favor to shift the burden of the obligation from off their own shoulders and place it in heaven, I had contrived to fix it on earth.

The last time I saw Mr. Whitefield was in London, when he consulted me about his orphan house concern and his purpose of appropriating it to the establishment of a college.

He had a loud and clear voice, and articulated his words so perfectly that he might be heard and understood at a great distance, especially as his auditors observed the most perfect silence. He preached one evening from the top of the court-house steps, which are in the middle of Market Street and on the west side of Second Street, which crosses it at right angles. Both streets were filled with his hearers to a considerable distance. Being among the hindmost in Market Street, I had the curiosity to learn how far he could be heard by retiring backward down the street toward the river; and I found his voice distinct till I came near Front Street, when some noise in that street obscured it. Imagining then a semicircle, of which my distance should be the radius, and that it was filled with auditors to each of whom I allowed two square feet, I computed that he might well be heard by more than thirty thousand. This reconciled me to the newspaper accounts of his having preached to twenty-five thousand people in the fields, and to the history of generals haranguing whole armies, of which I had sometimes doubted.[1]

By hearing him often I came to distinguish easily between sermons newly composed and those which he had often preached in the course of his travels. His delivery of the latter was so improved by frequent repetition that every accent, every emphasis, every modulation of voice, was so perfectly well turned and well placed that without being interested in the subject one could not help being pleased with the discourse; a pleasure of much the same kind with that received from an excellent piece of music. This is an advantage itinerant preachers have over those who are stationary, as the latter cannot well improve their delivery of a sermon by so many rehearsals.

His writing and printing from time to time gave great advantage to his enemies; unguarded expressions, and even erroneous opinions, delivered in preaching might have been afterward explained or qualified by supposing others that might have accompanied them; or they might have been denied; but *litera scripta manet*. Critics attacked his writings violently, and with so much appearance of reason as to diminish the number of his votaries and prevent their increase. So that I am satisfied that if he had never written anything he would have left behind him a much more numerous and important sect; and his reputation might in that case have been still growing even after his death, as there being nothing of his writing on which to found a censure and give him a lower character, his proselytes would be left at liberty to attribute to him as great a variety of excellences as their enthusiastic admiration might wish him to have possessed.

My business was now constantly augmenting and my circumstance growing daily easier, my newspaper having become very profitable, as being for a time almost the only one in this and the neighboring provinces. I experienced, too, the truth of the observation that *"after getting the first hundred pounds it is more easy to get the second;"* money itself being of a prolific nature.

The partnership at Carolina having succeeded, I was encouraged to engage in others and to promote several of my workmen, who had behaved well, by establishing them in printing-houses in different colonies, on the same terms with that in Carolina. Most of them did well, being enabled at the end of our term, six years, to purchase the types of me and go on working for themselves, by which means several families were raised. Partnerships often finish in quarrels; but I was happy in this, that mine were all carried on and ended amicably, owing, I think, a good deal to the precaution of having very explicitly settled in our articles everything to be done by or expected from each partner, so that there was nothing to dispute, which precaution I would therefore recommend to all who enter into partnerships; for whatever esteem partners may have for and confidence in each other at the time of the contract, little jealousies and disgusts may arise, with ideas of inequality in the care and burden, business, etc., which are attended often with breach of friendship and of the connection, perhaps with lawsuits and other disagreeable consequences.

I had, on the whole, abundant reason to be satisfied with my being established in Pennsylvania. There were, however, some things that I regretted, there being no provision for defense nor for a complete education of youth; no militia nor any college. I therefore, in 1743, drew up a proposal for establishing an academy; and at that time, thinking the Rev. Richard Peters, who was out of employ, a fit person to superintend such an institution, I communicated the project to him; but he, having more profitable views in the service of the proprietors, which succeeded, declined the undertaking, and not knowing another at that time suitable for such a trust, I let the scheme lie awhile dormant, I succeeded better the next year, 1744, in proposing and establishing a philosophical society. The paper I wrote for that purpose will be found among my writings, if not lost with many others.

With respect to defense, Spain having been several years at war against Great Britain and being at length joined by France, which brought us into great danger, and the labored and long-continued endeavor of our governor, Thomas, to prevail with our Quaker Assembly to pass a militia law and make other provisions for the security of the province having proved abortive, I proposed to try what might be done by a voluntary subscription of the people. To promote this I first wrote and published a pamphlet, entitled *Plain Truth,* in which I stated our helpless situation in strong lights, with the necessity of union and discipline for our defense, and promised to propose in a few days an association, to be generally signed for that purpose. The pamphlet had a sudden and surprising effect. I was called upon for the instrument of association. Having settled the draft of it with a few friends, I appointed a meeting of the citizens in the large building before mentioned. The house was pretty full. I had prepared a number of printed copies and provided pens and ink dispersed all over the room; I harangued them a little on the subject, read the paper, explained it, and then distributed the copies, which were eagerly signed, not the least objection being made.

When the company separated and the papers were collected, we found about twelve hundred signatures; and other copies being dispersed in the country, the subscribers amounted at length to upward of ten thousand. These all furnished themselves as soon as they could with arms, formed themselves into companies and regiments, chose their own officers, and met every week to be instructed in the manual exercise and other parts of military discipline. The women, by subscriptions among themselves, provided silk colors, which they presented to the companies, painted with different devices and mottoes, which I supplied.[2]

The officers of the companies composing the Philadelphia regiment being met, chose me for their colonel, but conceiving myself unfit I declined that station and recommended Mr. Lawrence, a fine person and a man of influence, who was accordingly appointed. I then proposed a lottery to defray the expense of building a battery below the town and furnished with cannon. It filled expeditiously and the battery was soon erected, the merlons being framed of logs and filled with earth. We bought some old cannon from Boston; but these not being sufficient, we wrote to London for more, soliciting at the same time our proprietaries for some assistance, though without much expectation of obtaining it.

Meanwhile Colonel Lawrence, Mr. Allan, Abraham Taylor, and myself were sent to New York by the associators, commissioned to borrow some cannon of Governor Clinton. He at first refused us peremptorily; but at a dinner with his Council, where there was great drinking of Madeira wine, as the custom of that place then was, he softened by degrees and said he would lend us six. After a few more bumpers he advanced to ten, and at length he very good-naturedly conceded eighteen. They were fine cannon, eighteen-pounders, with their carriages, which were soon transported and mounted on our batteries, where the associators kept a nightly guard while the war lasted, and among the rest I regularly took my turn of duty there as a common soldier.

My activity in these operations was agreeable to the governor and Council; they took me into confidence and I was consulted by them in every measure where their concurrence was thought useful to the association. Calling in the aid of religion, I proposed to them the proclaiming a fast, to promote reformation and implore the blessing of Heaven on our undertaking. They embraced the motion, but as it was the first fast ever thought of in the province, the secretary had no precedent from which to draw the proclamation. My education in New England, where a fast is proclaimed every year, was here of some advantage. I drew it in the accustomed style; it was translated into German, printed in both languages, and circulated through the province. This gave the clergy of the different sects an opportunity of influencing their congregations to join the association, and it would probably have been general among all but the Quakers if the peace had not soon intervened.

It was thought by some of my friends that by my activity in these affairs I should offend that sect, and thereby lose my interest in the Assembly of the province, where they formed a great majority. A young man, who had likewise some friends in the Assembly and wished to succeed me as their clerk, acquainted me that it was decided to displace me at the next election; and he, through good will, advised me to resign as more consistent with my honor than being turned out. My answer to him was that I had read or heard of some public man who made it a rule never to ask for an office and never to refuse one when offered to him. "I approve," said I, "of this rule, and shall practice it with a small addition: I shall never *ask*, never *refuse*, nor ever RESIGN an office. If they will have my office of clerk to dispose of it to another, they shall take it from me. I will not, by giving it up, lose my right of some time or other making reprisal of my adversaries." I heard, however, no more of this; I was chosen again unanimously as clerk at the next election. Possibly, as they disliked my late intimacy with the members of the Council who had joined the governors in all the disputes about military preparations with which the House had long been harassed, they might have been pleased if I would voluntarily have left them; but they did not care to displace me on account merely of my zeal for the association, and they could not well give another reason.

Indeed, I had some cause to believe that the defense of the country was not disagreeable to any of them, provided they were not required to assist in it. And I found that a much greater number of them than I could have imagined, though against *offensive* war, were clearly for the *defensive*. Many pamphlets *pro* and *con* were published on the subject, and some by good Quakers, in favor of *defense;* which, I believe, convinced most of their young people.

A transaction in our fire company gave me some insight into their prevailing sentiments. It had been proposed that we should encourage the scheme for building a battery by laying out the present stock, then about sixty pounds, in tickets of the lottery. By our rules no money could be disposed of till the next meeting after the proposal. The company consisted of thirty members, of whom twenty-two were Quakers and eight only of other persuasions. We eight punctually attended the meetings, but though we thought some of the Quakers would join us, we were by no means sure of a majority. Only one Quaker, Mr. James Morris, appeared to oppose the measure. He expressed much sorrow that it had ever been proposed, as he said *Friends* were all against it, and it would create such discord as might break up the company. We told him that we saw no reason for that; we were the minority, and if *Friends* were against the measure and outvoted us, we must and should, agreeably to the usage of all societies, submit. When the hour for business arrived it was moved to put this to the vote; he allowed we might do it by the rule, but as he could assure us that a number of members intended to be present for the purpose of opposing it, it would be but candid to allow a little time for their appearing.

While we were disputing this a waiter came to tell me that two gentlemen below desired to speak with me. I went down and found there two of our Quaker members. They told me there were eight of them assembled at a tavern just by; that they were determined to come and vote with us if there should be occasion, which they hoped would not be the case, and desired we would not call for their assistance if we could do without it, as their voting for such a measure might embroil them with their elders and friends. Being thus secure of a majority, I went up, and after a little seeming hesitation agreed to a delay of another hour. This Mr. Morris allowed to be extremely fair. Not one of his opposing friends appeared, at which he expressed great surprise, and at the expiration of the hour we carried the resolution eight to one; and as of the twenty-two Quakers eight were ready to vote with us and thirteen by their absence manifested that they were not inclined to oppose the measure, I afterward estimated the proportion of Quakers sincerely against defense as one to twenty-one only. For these were all regular members of the society and in good reputation among them, and who had notice of what was proposed at that meeting.

The honorable and learned Mr. Logan, who had always been of that sect, wrote an address to them, declaring his approbation of *defensive* war, and supported his opinion by many strong arguments. He put into my hands sixty pounds to be laid out in lottery tickets for the battery, with directions to apply what prizes might be drawn wholly to that service. He told me the following anecdote of his old master, William Penn, respecting defense. He came over from England when a young man with that proprietary, and as his secretary. It was war time, and their ship was chased by an armed vessel, supposed to be an enemy. Their captain prepared for defense, but told William Penn and his company of Quakers that he did not expect their assistance, and they might retire into the cabin, which they did, except James Logan, who chose to stay upon deck and was quartered to a gun. The supposed enemy proved a friend, so there was no fighting; but when the secretary went down to communicate the intelligence, William Penn rebuked him severely for staying upon deck and undertaking to assist in defending the vessel, contrary to the principles of Friends, especially as it had not been required by the captain. This reprimand, being before all the company, piqued the secretary, who answered: "I being thy servant, why did thee not order me to come down? But thee was willing enough that I should stay and help to fight the ship when thee thought there was danger."

My being many years in the Assembly, a majority of which was constantly Quakers, gave me frequent opportunities of seeing the embarrassment given them by their principle against war whenever application was made to them, by order of the crown, to grant aids for military purposes. They were unwilling to offend government, on the one hand, by a direct refusal, and their friends, the body of the Quakers, on the other, by a compliance contrary to their principles, using a variety of evasions to avoid complying and modes of disguising the compliance when it became unavoidable. The common mode at last was to grant money under the phrase of its being *"for the king's use,"* and never to inquire how it was applied.

But if the demand was not directly from the crown, that phrase was found not so proper, and some other was to be invented. Thus when powder was wanted (I think it was for the garrison at Louisburg) and the government at New England solicited a grant of some from Pennsylvania, which was much urged on the House by Governor Thomas, they would not grant money to buy *powder,* because that was an ingredient of war, but they voted an aid to New England of three thousand pounds, to be put into the hand of the governor, and appropriated it for the purchase of bread, flour, wheat, or *other grain.* Some of the Council, desirous of giving the House still further embarrassment, advised the governor not to accept that provision, as not being the thing he had demanded, but he replied, "I shall take the money, for I understand very well their meaning; *other grain* is gun-powder;" which he accordingly bought, and they never objected to it.

It was in allusion to this fact that, when in our fire company we feared the success of our proposal in favor of the lottery, and I had said to a friend of mine, one of our members, "If we fail let us move the purchase of a fire engine with the money, the Quakers can have no objection to that; and then, if you nominate me and I you as a committee for that purpose, we will buy a great gun, which is certainly a *fire engine.* " "I see," said he, "you have improved by being so long in the Assembly; your equivocal project would be just a match for their wheat or *other grain.* "

Those embarrassments that the Quakers suffered, from having established and published it as one of their principles that no kind of war was lawful, and which, being once published, they could not afterward, however they might change their minds, easily get rid of, reminds me of what I think a more prudent conduct in another sect among us, that of the Dunkers. I was acquainted with one of its founders, Michael Weffare, soon after it appeared. He complained to me that they were grievously calumniated by the zealots of other persuasions, and charged with abominable principles and practices to which they were utter strangers. I told him this had always been the case with new sects, and that to put a stop to such abuse I imagined it might be well to publish the articles of their belief and the rules of their discipline. He said that it had been proposed among them, but not agreed to for this reason: "When we were first drawn together as a society," said he, "it had pleased God to enlighten our minds so far as to see that some doctrines which were esteemed truths were errors, and that others which we had esteemed errors were real truths. From time to time he has been pleased to afford us further light, and our principles have been improving and our errors diminishing. Now we are not sure that we are arrived at the end of this progression and at the perfection of spiritual or theological knowledge, and we fear that if we should once print our confession of faith, we should feel ourselves as if bound and confined by it, and perhaps be unwilling to receive further improvement, and our successors still more so, as conceiving what their elders and founders had done to be something sacred—never to be departed from."

This modesty in a sect is perhaps a single instance in the history of mankind, every other sect supposing itself in possession of all truth, and that those who differ are so far in the wrong; like a man traveling in foggy weather, those at some distance before him on the road he sees wrapped up in the fog as well as those behind him, and also the people in the fields on each side, but near him all appears clear, though, in truth, he is as much in the fog as any of them. To avoid this kind of embarrassment, the Quakers have of late years been gradually declining the public service in the Assembly and in the magistracy, choosing rather to quit their power than their principle.

In order of time I should have mentioned before that having, in 1742, invented an open stove for the better warming of rooms, and at the same time saving fuel, as the fresh air was warmed in entering, I made a present of the model to Mr. Robert Grace, one of my early friends, who having an iron furnace found the casting of the plates for these stoves a profitable thing, as they were growing in demand. To promote that demand I wrote and published a pamphlet entitled *An Account of the new-invented Pennsylvanian Fireplaces, wherein their Construction and Manner of Operation are particularly explained, their advantages above every other Method of Warming Rooms demonstrated, and all Objections that have been raised against the Use of them answered and obviated,* etc. This pamphlet had a good effect. Governor Thomas was so pleased with the construction of this stove, as described in it, that he offered to give me a patent for the sole vending of them for a term of years, but I declined it from a principle which has ever weighed with me on such occasions, viz., *that as we enjoy great advantages from the inventions of others, we should be glad of an opportunity to serve others by any invention of ours, and this we should do freely and generously.*

An ironmonger in London, however, assuming a good deal of my pamphlet and working it up into his own, and making some small changes in the machine, which rather hurt its operation, got a patent for it there, and made, as I was told, a little fortune by it. And this is not the only instance of patents taken out of my inventions by others, though not always with the same success; which I never contested, as having no desire of profiting by patents myself and hating disputes. The use of these fire-places in very many houses, both here in Pennsylvania and the neighboring States, has been and is a great saving of wood to the inhabitants.

CHAPTER IX

PEACE being concluded and the association business therefore at an end, I turned my thoughts again to the affair of establishing an academy. The first step I took was to associate in the design a number of active friends, of whom the Junto furnished a good part; the next was to write and publish a pamphlet, entitled *Proposals relating to the Education of Youth in Pennsylvania.* This I distributed among the principal inhabitants gratis; and as soon as I could suppose their minds a little prepared by the perusal of it, I set on foot a subscription for opening and supporting an academy; it was to be paid in quotas yearly for five years. By so dividing it I judged the subscription might be larger; and I believe it was so, amounting to no less, if I remember right, than five thousand pounds.

In the introduction to these proposals I stated their publication not as an act of mine, but of some *public spirited gentlemen;* avoiding as much as I could, according to my usual rule, the presenting myself to the public as the author of any scheme for their benefit.

The subscribers, to carry the project into immediate execution, chose out of their number twenty-four trustees, and appointed Mr. Francis, then Attorney-General, and myself, to draw up constitutions for the government of the academy; which being done and signed, a house was hired, masters engaged, and the schools opened, I think in the same year, 1749.

The scholars increasing fast, the house was soon found too small, and we were looking out for a piece of ground, properly situated, with intent to build, when accident threw into our way a large house ready built, which, with a few alterations, might well serve our purpose. This was the building before mentioned, erected by the hearers of Mr. Whitefield, and was obtained for us in the following manner.

It is to be noted that the contributions to this building being made by people of different sects, care was taken in the nomination of trustees in whom the building and ground were to be vested, that a predominancy should not be given to any sect, lest in time that predominancy might be a means of appropriating the whole to the use of such sect, contrary to the original intention. It was for this reason that one of each sect was appointed, viz., one Church of England man, one Presbyterian, one Baptist, one Moravian, etc., who, in case of vacancy by death, were to fill it by election from among the contributors. The Moravian happened not to please his colleagues, and on his death they resolved to have no other of that sect. The difficulty then was how to avoid having two of some other sect, by means of the choice.

Several persons were named, and for that reason not agreed to. At length one mentioned me, with the observation that I was merely an honest man, and of *no sect* at all, which prevailed with them to choose me. The enthusiasm which existed when the house was built had long since abated, and its trustees had not been able to procure fresh contributions for paying the ground-rent and discharging some other debts the building had occasioned, which embarrassed them greatly. Being now a member of both boards of trustees, that for the building and that for the academy, I had a good opportunity for negotiating with both, and brought them finally to an agreement by which the trustees for the building were to cede it to those of the academy; the latter undertaking to discharge the debt, to keep forever open in the building a large hall for occasional preachers, according to the original intention, and maintain a free school for the instruction of poor children. Writings were accordingly drawn; and on paying the debts the trustees of the academy were put in possession of the premises, and by dividing the great and lofty hall into stories and different rooms above and below for the several schools, and purchasing some additional ground, the whole was soon made fit for our purpose and the scholars removed into the building. The whole care and trouble of agreeing with the workman, purchasing materials, and superintending the work fell upon me; and I went through it the more cheerfully as it did not then interfere with my private business, having the year before taken a very able, industrious, and honest partner, Mr. David Hall, with whose character I was well acquainted, as he had worked for me four years. He took off my hands all care of the printing-office, paying me punctually my share of the profits. This partnership continued eighteen years, successfully for us both.

The trustees of the academy, after awhile, were incorporated by a charter from the governor; their funds were increased by contributions in Britain and grants of land from the proprietaries, to which the Assembly has since made considerable addition; and thus was established the present University of Philadelphia. I have been continued one of its trustees from the beginning, now near forty years, and have had the very great pleasure of seeing a number of the youth who have received their education in it distinguished by their improved abilities, serviceable in public stations, and ornaments to their country.

When I was disengaged myself, as above mentioned, from private business, I flattered myself that by the sufficient though moderate fortune I had acquired I had found leisure during the rest of my life for philosophical studies and amusements. I purchased all Dr. Spence's apparatus, who had come from England to lecture in Philadelphia, and I proceeded in my electrical experiments with great alacrity; but the public, now considering me as a man of leisure, laid hold of me for their purposes, every part of our civil government, and almost at the same time, imposing some duty upon me. The governor put me into the commission of the peace; the corporation of the city chose me one of the Common Council and soon after alderman; and the citizens at large elected me a burgess to represent them in the Assembly. This latter station was the more agreeable to me, as I grew at length tired with sitting there to hear the debates, in which, as clerk, I could take no part, and which were often so uninteresting that I was induced to amuse myself with making magic squares or circles, or anything to avoid weariness; and I conceived my becoming a member would enlarge my power of doing good. I would not, however, insinuate that my ambition was not flattered by all these promotions; it certainly was, for considering my low beginning they were great things to me, and they were still more pleasing as being so many spontaneous testimonies of the public good opinion, and by me entirely unsolicited.

The office of justice of the peace I tried a little by attending a few courts and sitting on the bench to hear causes; but finding that more knowledge of the common law than I possessed was necessary to act in that station with credit, I gradually withdrew from it, excusing myself by being obliged to attend the higher duties of a legislator in the Assembly. My election to this trust was repeated every year for ten years, without my ever asking any elector for his vote or signifying, either directly or indirectly, any desire of being chosen. On taking my seat in the House my son was appointed their clerk.

The year following, a treaty being to be held with the Indians at Carlisle, the governor sent a message to the House proposing that they should nominate some of their members, to be joined with some members of Council, as commissioners for that purpose. The House named the Speaker (Mr. Norris) and myself, and being commissioned we went to Carlisle and met the Indians accordingly.

As those people are extremely apt to get drunk, and when so are very quarrelsome and disorderly, we strictly forbade the selling any liquor to them; and when they complained of this restriction, we told them that if they would continue sober during the treaty we would give them plenty of rum when the business was over. They promised this, and they kept their promise, because they could get no rum; and the treaty was conducted very orderly and concluded to mutual satisfaction. They then claimed and received the rum; this was in the afternoon. They were near one hundred men, women, and children, and were lodged in temporary cabins, built in the form of a square, just without the town. In the evening, hearing a great noise among them, the commissioners walked to see what was the matter. We found they had made a great bonfire in the middle of the square; they were all drunk, men and women, quarreling and fighting. Their dark-colored bodies, half-naked, seen only by the gloomy light of the bonfire, running after and beating one another with fire-brands, accompanied by their horrid yellings, formed a scene the most resembling our ideas of hell that could well be imagined! There was no appeasing the tumult, and we retired to our lodging. At midnight a number of them came thundering at our door, demanding more rum, of which we took no notice.

The next day, sensible they had misbehaved in giving us that disturbance, they sent three of their old counselors to make their apology. The orator acknowledged the fault, but laid it upon the rum; and then endeavored to excuse the rum by saying: "The Great Spirit, who made all things, made everything for some use; and whatever use he designed anything for, that use it should always be put to. Now, when he made rum, he said, '*Let this be for the Indians to get drunk with*'; and it must be so." And, indeed, if it be the design of Providence to extirpate these savages in order to make room for the cultivators of the earth, it seems not impossible that rum may be the appointed means. It has already annihilated all the tribes who formerly inhabited the sea-coast.

In 1751 Dr. Thomas Bond, a particular friend of mine, conceived the idea of establishing a hospital in Philadelphia (a very beneficent design, which has been ascribed to me, but was originally and truly his) for the reception and cure of poor sick persons, whether inhabitants of the province or strangers. He was zealous and active in endeavoring to procure subscriptions for it; but the proposal being a novelty in America, and at first not well understood, he met but with little success.

At length he came to me with the compliment that he found there was no such a thing as carrying a public-spirited project through without my being concerned in it. "For," said he, "I am often asked by those to whom I propose subscribing, *'Have you consulted Franklin on this business? And what does he think of it?'* And when I tell them that I have not, supposing it rather out of your line, they do not subscribe, but say, *They will consider it.*" I inquired into the nature and probable utility of this scheme, and receiving from him a very satisfactory explanation, I not only subscribed to it myself, but engaged heartily in the design of procuring subscriptions from others. Previously, however, to the solicitation, I endeavored to prepare the minds of the people by writing on the subject in the newspapers, which was my usual custom in such cases, but which Dr. Bond had omitted.

The subscriptions afterward were more free and generous; but, beginning to flag, I saw they would be insufficient without some assistance from the Assembly, and therefore proposed to petition for it, which was done. The country members did not at first relish the project. They objected that it could only be serviceable to the city, and therefore the citizens alone should be at the expense of it; and they doubted whether the citizens themselves generally approved of it. My allegation, on the contrary, that it met with such approbation as to leave no doubt of our being able to raise two thousand pounds by voluntary donations, they considered as a most extravagant supposition and utterly impossible.

On this I formed my plan; and asking leave to bring in a bill for incorporating the contributors according to the prayer of their petition and granting them a blank sum of money, which leave was obtained chiefly on the consideration that the House could throw the bill out if they did not like it, I drew it so as to make the important clause a conditional one, viz.: "And be it enacted by the authority aforesaid, that when the said contributors shall have met and chosen their managers and treasurer, and shall have raised by their contributions a capital stock of two thousand pounds' value (the yearly interest of which is to be applied to the accommodation of the sick poor in the said hospital, and of charge for diet, attendance, advice, and medicines), and *shall make the same appear to the satisfaction of the Speaker of the Assembly for the time being,* that then it shall and may be lawful for the said Speaker, and he is hereby required to sign an order on the provincial treasurer for the payment of two thousand pounds, in two yearly payments, to the treasurer of the said hospital, to be applied to the founding, building, and finishing of the same."

This condition carried the bill through; for the members who had opposed the grant and now conceived they might have the credit of being charitable without the expense agreed to its passage. And then, in soliciting subscriptions among the people, we urged the conditional promise of the law as an additional motive to give, since every man's donation would be doubled; thus the clause worked both ways. The subscriptions accordingly soon exceeded the requisite sum, and we claimed and received the public gift, which enabled us to carry the design into execution. A convenient and handsome building was soon erected; the institution has by constant experience been found useful and flourishes to this day; and I do not remember any of my political maneuvers the success of which at the time gave me more pleasure, or wherein, after thinking of it, I more easily excused myself for having made some use of cunning.

It was about this time that another projector, the Rev. Gilbert Tennent, came to me with a request that I would assist him in procuring a subscription for erecting a new meeting-house. It was to be for the use of a congregation he had gathered among the Presbyterians who were originally disciples of Mr. Whitefield. Unwilling to make myself disagreeable to my fellow-citizens by too frequently soliciting their contribution, I absolutely refused. He then desired I would furnish him with the list of the names of persons I knew by experience to be generous and public-spirited. I thought it would be unbecoming in me, after their kind compliance with my solicitations, to mark them out to be worried by other beggars, and therefore refused to give such a list. He then desired I would at least give him my advice. "That I will readily do," said I; "and, in the first place, I advise you to apply to all those who you know will give something; next, to those who you are uncertain whether they will give anything or not, and show them the list of those who have given; and lastly, do not neglect those who you are sure will give nothing; for in some of them you may be mistaken." He laughed and thanked me, and he said he would take my advice. He did so, for he asked of *everybody;* and he obtained a much larger sum than he expected, with which he erected the capacious and elegant meeting-house that stands in Arch Street.

Our city, though laid out with a beautiful regularity, the streets large, straight, and crossing each other at right angles, had the disgrace of suffering those streets to remain long unpaved, and in wet weather the wheels of heavy carriages plowed them into a quagmire, so that it was difficult to cross them; and in dry weather the dust was offensive. I had lived near what was called the Jersey Market, and saw with pain the inhabitants wading in mud while purchasing their provisions. A strip of ground down the middle of that market was at length paved with brick, so that being once in the market they had firm footing; but were often over shoes in dirt to get there. By talking and writing on the subject, I was at length instrumental in getting the street paved with stone between the market and the brick foot pavement, that was on the side next the houses. This for some time gave an easy access to the market dryshod; but the rest of the street not being paved, whenever a carriage came out of the mud upon this pavement it shook off and left its dirt upon it, and it was soon covered with mire, which was not removed, the city as yet having no scavengers.

After some inquiry I found a poor, industrious man, who was willing to undertake keeping the pavement clean by sweeping it twice a week, carrying off the dirt from before all the neighbors' doors, for the sum of sixpence per month, to be paid by each house. I then wrote and printed a paper setting forth the advantages to the neighborhood that might be obtained from this small expense; the greater ease in keeping our houses clean, so much dirt not being brought in by people's feet; the benefit to the shops by more custom, as buyers could more easily get at them; and by not having in windy weather the dust blown in upon their goods, etc., etc. I sent one of these papers to each house, and in a day or two went round to see who would subscribe an agreement to pay these sixpences; it was unanimously signed and for a time well executed. All the inhabitants of the city were delighted with the cleanliness of the pavement that surrounded the market, it being a convenience to all, and this raised a general desire to have all the streets paved and made the people more willing to submit to a tax for that purpose.

After some time I drew a bill for paving the city and brought it into the Assembly. It was just before I went to England, in 1757, and did not pass till I was gone, and then with an alteration in the mode of assessment which I thought not for the better, but with an additional provision for lighting as well as paving the streets, which was a great improvement. It was by a private person, the late Mr. John Clifton, giving a sample of the utility of lamps, by placing one at his door, that the people were first impressed with the idea of lighting all the city. The honor of this public benefit has also been ascribed to me, but it belongs truly to that gentleman. I did but follow his example, and have only some merit to claim respecting the form of our lamps, as differing from the globe lamps we were at first supplied with from London. They were found inconvenient in these respects: they admitted no air below; the smoke therefore did not readily go out above, but circulated in the globe, lodged on its inside, and soon obstructed the light they were intended to afford; giving besides the daily trouble of wiping them clean; and an accidental stroke on one of them would demolish it and render it totally useless. I therefore suggested the composing them of four flat panes, with a long funnel above to draw up the smoke, and crevices admitting the air below to facilitate the ascent of the smoke; by this means they were kept clean and did not grow dark in a few hours, as the London lamps do, but continued bright till morning; and an accidental stroke would generally break but a single pane, easily repaired.

I have sometimes wondered that the Londoners did not, from the effect holes in the bottom of the globe lamps used at Vauxhall have in keeping them clean, learn to have such holes in their street lamps. But these holes being made for another purpose, viz., to communicate flame more suddenly to the wick by a little flax hanging down through them, the other use, of letting in air, seems not to have been thought of; and therefore after the lamps have been lit a few hours the streets of London are very poorly illuminated.

The mention of these improvements puts me in mind of one I proposed, when in London, to Dr. Fothergill, who was among the best men I have known, and a great promoter of useful projects. I had observed that the streets, when dry, were never swept and the light dust carried away, but it was suffered to accumulate till wet weather reduced it to mud; and then, after lying some days so deep on the pavement that there was no crossing but in paths kept clean by poor people with brooms, it was with great labor raked together and thrown up into carts, open above, the sides of which suffered some of the slush at every jolt on the pavement to shake out and fall; sometimes to the annoyance of foot passengers. The reason given for not sweeping the dusty streets was that the dust would fly into the windows of shops and houses.

An accidental occurrence had instructed me how much sweeping might be done in a little time. I found at my door in Craven Street, one morning, a poor woman sweeping my pavement with a birch broom; she appeared very pale and feeble, as just come out of a fit of sickness. I asked who employed her to sweep there; she said; "Nobody; but I am poor and in distress, and I sweeps before gentle folkses' doors and hopes they will give me something." I bid her sweep the whole street clean and I would give her a shilling; this was at nine o'clock, and at noon she came for the shilling. From the slowness I saw at first in her working I could scarce believe that the work was done so soon, and sent my servant to examine it, who reported that the whole street was swept perfectly clean and all the dust placed in the gutter, which was in the middle; and the next rain washed it quite away, so that the pavement and even the kennel were perfectly clean.

I then judged that if that feeble woman could sweep such a street in three hours, a strong, active man might have done it in half the time. And here let me remark the convenience of having but one gutter in such a narrow street, running down its middle, instead of two, one on each side near the footway. For where all the rain that falls on a street runs from the sides and meets in the middle, it forms there a current strong enough to wash away all the mud it meets with; but when divided into two channels, it is often too weak to cleanse either and only makes the mud it finds more fluid; so that the wheels of carriages and feet of horses throw and dash it upon the foot pavement, which is thereby rendered foul and slippery, and sometimes splash it upon those who are walking. My proposal, communicated to the doctor, was as follows:

"For the more effectually cleaning and keeping clean the streets of London and Westminster, it is proposed that the several watchmen be contracted with to have the dust swept up in dry seasons and the mud raked up at other times, each in the several streets and lanes of his round; that they be furnished with brooms and other proper instruments for these purposes, to be kept at their respective stands, ready to furnish the poor people they may employ in the service.

"That in the dry summer months the dust be all swept up into heaps at proper distances, before the shops and windows of houses are usually opened, when scavengers with close-covered carts shall also carry it all away.

"That the mud, when raked up, be not left in heaps to be spread abroad again by the wheels of carriages and trampling of horses, but that the scavengers be provided with bodies of carts, not placed upon wheels, but low upon sliders, with lattice bottoms, which, being covered with straw, will retain the mud thrown upon them and permit the water to drain from it; whereby it will become much lighter, water making the greatest part of the weight. These bodies of carts to be placed at convenient distances and the mud brought to them in wheelbarrows, they remaining where placed till the mud is drained, and then horses brought to draw them away."

I have since had doubts of the practicability of the latter part of this proposal in all places, on account of the narrowness of some streets and the difficulty of placing the draining sleds so as not to incumber too much the passage; but I am still of opinion that the former, requiring the dust to be swept up and carried away before the shops are open, is very practicable in the summer, when the days are long; for in walking through the Strand and Fleet Street one morning at seven o'clock, I observed there was not one shop open, though it had been daylight and the sun up above three hours; the inhabitants of London choosing voluntarily to live much by candlelight and sleep by sunshine, and yet often complain, a little absurdly, of the duty on candles and the high price of tallow.

Some may think these trifling matters not worth minding or relating; but when they consider that though dust blown into the eyes of a single person or into a single shop in a windy day is but of small importance, yet the great number of the instances in a populous city and its frequent repetition gives its weight and consequence, perhaps they will not censure very severely those who bestow some attention to affairs of this seemingly low nature. Human felicity is produced not so much by great pieces of good fortune that seldom happen as by little advantages that occur every day. Thus if you teach a poor young man to shave himself and keep his razor in order, you may contribute more to the happiness of his life than in giving him a thousand guineas. This sum may be soon spent, the regret only remaining of having foolishly consumed it; but in the other case he escapes the frequent vexation of waiting for barbers and their sometimes dirty fingers, offensive breaths, and dull razors; he shaves when most convenient to him, and enjoys daily the pleasure of its being done with a good instrument. With these sentiments I have hazarded the few preceding pages, hoping they may afford hints which some time or other may be useful to a city I love, having lived many years in it very happily, and perhaps to some of our towns in America.

Having been some time employed by the Postmaster-General of America as his comptroller in regulating several offices and bringing the officers to account, I was, upon his death in 1753, appointed, jointly with Mr. William Hunter, to succeed him, by a commission from the Postmaster-General in England. The American office had hitherto never paid anything to that of Britain. We were to have six hundred pounds a year between us if we could make that sum out of the profits of the office. To do this a variety of improvements were necessary; some of these were inevitably at first expensive; so that in the first four years the office became about nine hundred pounds in debt to us. But it soon after began to repay us, and before I was displaced by a freak of the ministers, of which I shall speak hereafter, we had brought it to yield *three times* as much clear revenue to the crown as the post-office of Ireland. Since that imprudent transaction they have received from it—not one farthing!

The business of the post-office occasioned my taking a journey this year to New England, where the College of Cambridge, of their own motion, presented me with the degree of Master of Arts. Yale College in Connecticut had before made me a similar compliment. Thus without studying in any college I came to partake of their honors. They were conferred in consideration of my improvements and discoveries in the electric branch of natural philosophy.

CHAPTER X

IN 1754, war with France being again apprehended, a congress of commissioners from the different colonies was by an order of the Lords of Trade to be assembled at Albany, there to confer with the chiefs of the Six Nations concerning the means of defending both their country and ours. Governor Hamilton having received this order acquainted the House with it, requesting they would furnish proper presents for the Indians, to be given on this occasion; and naming the Speaker (Mr. Norris) and myself to join Mr. John Penn and Mr. Secretary Peters as commissioners to act for Pennsylvania. The House approved the nomination and provided the goods for the presents, though they did not much like treating out of the province; and we met the other commissioners at Albany about the middle of June.

In our way thither I projected and drew up a plan for the union of all the colonies under one government, so far as might be necessary for defense, and other important general purposes. As we passed through New York I had there shown my project to Mr. James Alexander and Mr. Kennedy, two gentlemen of great knowledge in public affairs; and being fortified by their approbation, I ventured to lay it before the congress. It then appeared that several of the commissioners had formed plans of the same kind. A previous question was first taken, whether a union should be established, which passed in the affirmative unanimously. A committee was then appointed, one member from each colony, to consider the several plans and report. Mine happened to be preferred and, with a few amendments, was accordingly reported.

By this plan the general government was to be administered by a president-general, appointed and supported by the crown, and a grand council was to be chosen by the representatives of the people of the several colonies met in their respective assemblies. The debates upon it in the congress went on daily, hand in hand with the Indian business. Many objections and difficulties were started; but at length they were all overcome and the plan was unanimously agreed to, and copies ordered to be transmitted to the Board of Trade and to the Assemblies of the several provinces. Its fate was singular; the Assemblies did not adopt it, as they all thought there was too much *prerogative* in it; and in England it was judged to have too much of the *democratic*. The Board of Trade did not approve it nor recommend it for the approbation of his majesty; but another scheme was formed, supposed to answer the same purpose better, whereby the governors of the provinces, with some members of their respective councils, were to meet and order the raising of troops, building of forts, etc., and to draw on the treasury of Great Britain for the expense, which was afterward to be refunded by an act of Parliament laying a tax on America. My plan, with my reasons in support of it, is to be found among my political papers that were printed.

Being the winter following in Boston, I had much conversation with Governor Shirley upon both the plans. Part of what passed between us on this occasion may also be seen among those papers. The different and contrary reasons of dislike to my plan make me suspect that it was really the true medium, and I am still of opinion it would have been happy for both sides if it had been adopted. The colonies so united would have been sufficiently strong to have defended themselves; there would then have been no need of troops from England; of course the subsequent pretext for taxing America and the bloody contest it occasioned would have been avoided. But such mistakes are not new; history is full of the errors of states and princes.

"Look round the habitable world; how few
Know their own good, or, knowing it, pursue!"

Those who govern, having much business on their hands, do not generally like to take the trouble of considering and carrying into execution new projects. The best public measures are therefore seldom adopted from previous wisdom, but forced by the occasion.

The Governor of Pennsylvania, in sending it down to the Assembly, expressed his approbation of the plan, "as appearing to him to be drawn up with great clearness and strength of judgment, and therefore recommended it as well worthy of their closest and most serious attention." The House, however, by the management of a certain member, took it up when I happened to be absent, which I thought not very fair, and reprobated it without paying any attention to it at all, to my no small mortification.

In my journey to Boston this year I met at New York with our new governor, Mr. Morris, just arrived there from England, with whom I had been before intimately acquainted. He brought a commission to supersede Mr. Hamilton, who, tired with the disputes his proprietary instructions subjected him to, had resigned. Mr. Morris asked me if I thought he must expect as uncomfortable an administration. I said, "No; you may, on the contrary, have a very comfortable one if you will only take care not to enter into any dispute with the Assembly." "My dear friend," said he pleasantly, "how can you advise my avoiding disputes? You know I love disputing — it is one of my greatest pleasures; however, to show the regard I have for your counsel, I promise you I will, if possible, avoid them." He had some reason for loving to dispute; being eloquent, an acute sophister, and therefore generally successful in argumentative conversation. He had been brought up to it from a boy, his father, as I have heard, accustoming his children to dispute with one another for his diversion while sitting at table after dinner; but I think the practice was not wise, for in the course of my observation those disputing, contradicting, and confuting people are generally unfortunate in their affairs. They get victory sometimes, but they never get goodwill, which would be of more use to them. We parted, he going to Philadelphia and I to Boston.

In returning I met at New York with the votes of the Assembly of Pennsylvania, by which it appeared that notwithstanding his promise to me he and the House were already in high contention, and it was a continual battle between them as long as he retained the government. I had my share of it, for as soon as I got back to my seat in the Assembly I was put on every committee for answering his speeches and messages, and by the committees always desired to make the drafts. Our answers, as well as his messages, were often tart and sometimes indecently abusive, and as he knew I wrote for the Assembly, one might have imagined that when we met we could hardly avoid cutting throats; but he was so good-natured a man that no personal difference between him and me was occasioned by the contest, and we often dined together.

One afternoon, in the height of this public quarrel, we met in the street. "Franklin," said he, "you must go home with me and spend the evening. I am to have some company that you will like," and taking me by the arm led me to his house. In gay conversation over our wine after supper he told us, jokingly, that he much admired the idea of Sancho Panza, who, when it was proposed to give him a government, requested it might be a government of blacks, as then, if he could not agree with his people, he might sell them. One of his friends, who sat next to me, said: "Franklin, why do you continue to side with those damned Quakers? Had you not better sell them? The proprietor would give you a good price." "The governor," replied I, "has not yet *blacked* them enough." He, indeed, had labored hard to blacken the Assembly in all his messages, but they wiped off his coloring as fast as he laid it on, and placed it, in return, thick upon his own face, so that finding he was likely to be *negrofied* himself, he, as well as Mr. Hamilton, grew tired of the contest and quitted the government.

These public quarrels were all at bottom owing to the proprietaries, our hereditary governors, who, when any expense was to be incurred for the defense of their province, with incredible meanness instructed their deputies to pass no act for levying the necessary taxes unless their vast estates were in the same act expressly exonerated; and they had even taken the bonds of these deputies to observe such instructions. The Assemblies for three years held out against this injustice, though constrained to bend at last. At length Captain Denny, who was Governor Morris' successor, ventured to disobey those instructions: how that was brought about I shall show hereafter.

But I am got forward too fast with my story; there are still some transactions to be mentioned that happened during the administration of Governor Morris.

War being in a manner commenced with France, the government of Massachusetts Bay projected an attack upon Crown Point, and sent Mr. Quincy to Pennsylvania and Mr. Pownall, afterward Governor Pownall, to New York, to solicit assistance. As I was in the Assembly, knew its temper, and was Mr. Quincy's countryman, he applied to me for my influence and assistance. I dictated his address to them, which was well received. They voted an aid of ten thousand pounds, to be laid out in provisions. But the governor refusing his assent to their bill (which included this with other sums granted for the use of the crown) unless a clause were inserted exempting the proprietary estate from bearing any part of the tax that would be necessary, the Assembly, though very desirous of making their grant to New England effectual, were at a loss how to accomplish it. Mr. Quincy labored hard with the governor to obtain his assent, but he was obstinate.

I then suggested a method of doing the business without the governor, by orders on the trustees of the loan office, which by law the Assembly had the right of drawing. There was indeed little or no money at the time in the office, and therefore I proposed that the orders should be payable in a year and to bear an interest of five per cent. With these orders I supposed the provisions might easily be purchased. The Assembly, with very little hesitation, adopted the proposal. The orders were immediately printed, and I was one of the committee directed to sign and dispose of them. The fund for paying them was the interest of all the paper currency then extant in the province upon loan, together with the revenue arising from the excise, which being known to be more than sufficient, they obtained credit, and were not only taken in payment for the provisions, but many moneyed people who had cash lying by them vested it in those orders, which they found advantageous, as they bore interest while upon hand and might on any occasion be used as money; so that they were eagerly all bought up, and in a few weeks none of them was to be seen. Thus this important affair was by my means completed. Mr. Quincy returned thanks to the Assembly in a handsome memorial, went home highly pleased with the success of his embassy, and ever after bore for me the most cordial and affectionate friendship.

The British government, not choosing to permit the union of the colonies as proposed at Albany and to trust that union with their defense, lest they should thereby grow too military and feel their own strength, suspicion and jealousies at this time being entertained of them, sent over General Braddock, with two regiments of regular English troops for that purpose. He landed at Alexandria, in Virginia, and thence marched to Frederictown, in Maryland, where he halted for carriages. Our Assembly, apprehending from some information that he had conceived violent prejudices against them, as averse to the service, wished me to wait upon him, not as from them, but as Postmaster-General, under the guise of proposing to settle with him the mode of conducting with most celerity and certainty the dispatches between him and the governors of the several provinces, with whom he must necessarily have continual correspondence, and of which they proposed to pay the expense. My son accompanied me on this journey.

We found the general at Frederictown, waiting impatiently for the return of those he had sent through the back parts of Maryland and Virginia to collect wagons. I stayed with him several days, dined with him daily, and had full opportunities of removing his prejudices by the information of what the Assembly had before his arrival actually done, and were still willing to do, to facilitate his operations. When I was about to depart the returns of wagons to be obtained were brought in, by which it appeared that they amounted only to twenty-five, and not all of those were in serviceable condition. The general and all the officers were surprised, declared the expedition was then at an end, being impossible, and exclaimed against the ministers for ignorantly sending them into a country destitute of the means of conveying their stores, baggage, etc., not less than one hundred and fifty wagons being necessary.

I happened to say I thought it was a pity they had not been landed in Pennsylvania, as in that country almost every farmer had his wagon. The general eagerly laid hold of my words and said: "Then you, sir, who are a man of interest there, can probably procure them for us, and I beg you will undertake it." I asked what terms were to be offered the owners of the wagons, and I was desired to put on paper the terms that appeared to me necessary. This I did, and they were agreed to, and a commission and instructions accordingly prepared immediately. What those terms were will appear in the advertisement I published as soon as I arrived at Lancaster, which being, from the great and sudden effect it produced, a piece of some curiosity, I shall insert it at length as follows:

"ADVERTISEMENT.

"LANCASTER, April 26th, 1755.
"Whereas, one hundred and fifty wagons, with four horses to each wagon, and fifteen hundred saddle or pack horses, are wanted for the service of his majesty's forces, now about to ren-

dezvous at Will's Creek; and his excellency General Braddock having been pleased to empower me to contract for the hire of the same, I hereby give notice that I shall attend for that purpose, at Lancaster, from this day to next Wednesday evening; and at York, from next Thursday morning till Friday evening; where I shall be ready to agree for wagons and teams, or single horses, on the following terms, viz.: 1. That there shall be paid for each wagon, with four good horses and a driver, fifteen shillings *per diem;* and for each able horse with a pack-saddle, or other saddle and furniture, two shillings *per diem;* and for each able horse without a saddle, eighteen pence *per diem.* 2. That the pay commence from the time of their joining the forces, at Will's Creek, which must be on or before the 20th of May ensuing, and that a reasonable allowance be paid over and above for the time necessary for their traveling to Will's Creek and home again after their discharge. 3. Each wagon and team and every saddle or pack horse is to be valued by indifferent persons, chosen between me and the owner; and in case of the loss of any wagon, team, or other horse in the service, the price according to such valuation is to be allowed and paid. 4. Seven days' pay is to be advanced and paid in hand by me to the owner of each wagon and team or horse at the time of contracting, if required; and the remainder to be paid by General Braddock, or by the paymaster of the army, at the time of their discharge; or from time to time, as it shall be demanded. 5. No drivers of wagons, or persons taking care of the hired horses, are on any account to be called upon to do the duty of soldiers, or be otherwise employed than in conducting or taking care of their carriages or horses. 6. All oats, Indian corn, or other forage that wagons or horses bring to the camp more than is necessary for the subsistence of the horses is to be taken for the use of the army, and a reasonable price paid for the same.

"*Note.*—My son, William Franklin, is empowered to enter into like contracts with any person in Cumberland County.

"B. FRANKLIN."

"To the Inhabitants of the Counties of Lancaster, York, and Cumberland.

"FRIENDS AND COUNTRYMEN: Being occasionally at the camp at Frederic a few days since, I found the general and officers extremely exasperated on account of their not being supplied with horses and carriages, which had been expected from this province, as most able to furnish them; but through the dissensions between our governor and Assembly, money had not been provided nor any steps taken for that purpose.

"It was proposed to send an armed force immediately into these counties, to seize as many of the best carriages and horses as should be wanted, and compel as many persons into the service as would be necessary to drive and take care of them.

"I apprehended that the progress of British soldiers through these counties on such an occasion, especially considering the temper they are in and their resentment against us, would be attended with many and great inconveniences to the inhabitants, and therefore more willingly took the trouble of trying first what might be done by fair and equitable means. The people of these back counties have lately complained to the Assembly that a sufficient currency was wanting; you have an opportunity of receiving and dividing among you a considerable sum; for if the service of this expedition should continue, as it is more than probable it will, for one hundred and twenty days, the hire of these wagons and horses will amount to upward of thirty thousand pounds, which will be paid you in silver and gold of the king's money.

"The service will be light and easy, for the army will scarce march above twelve miles per day, and the wagons and baggage horses, as they carry those things that are absolutely necessary to the welfare of the army, must march with the army, and no faster; and are, for the army's sake, always placed where they can be most secure, whether in a march or in a camp.

"If you are really, as I believe you are, good and loyal subjects to his majesty, you may now do a most acceptable service and make it easy to yourselves; for three or four of such as cannot separately spare from the business of their plantations a wagon and four horses and a driver may do it together; one furnishing the wagon, another one or two horses, and another the driver, and divide the pay proportionately between you. But if you do not this service to your king and country voluntarily, when such good pay and reasonable terms are offered to you, your loyalty will be strongly suspected. The king's business must be done; so many brave troops, come so far for your defense, must not stand idle through your backwardness to do what may be reasonably expected from you; wagons and horses must be had; violent measures will probably be used; and you will be left to seek for a recompense where you can find it, and your case perhaps be little pitied or regarded.

"I have no particular interest in this affair, as, except the satisfaction of endeavoring to do good, I shall have only my labor for my pains. If this method of obtaining the wagons and horses is not likely to succeed, I am obliged to send word to the general in fourteen days; and I suppose Sir John St. Clair, the hussar with a body of soldiers, will immediately enter the province for the purpose; which I shall be sorry to hear, because I am very sincerely and truly your friend and well-wisher,

"B. FRANKLIN."

I received of the general about eight hundred pounds, to be disbursed in advance money to the wagon-owners; but that sum being insufficient, I advanced upward of two hundred pounds more; and in two weeks the one hundred and fifty wagons, with two hundred and fifty-nine carrying-horses, were on their march for the camp. The advertisement promised payment according to the valuation in case any wagons or horses should be lost. The owners, however, alleging they did not know General Braddock or what dependence might be had on his promise, insisted on my bond for the performance, which I accordingly gave them.

While I was at the camp supping one evening with the officers of Colonel Dunbar's regiment, he represented to me his concern for the subalterns, who, he said, were generally not in affluence, and could ill afford in this dear country to lay in the stores that might be necessary in so long a march through a wilderness where nothing was to be purchased. I commiserated their case and resolved to endeavor procuring them some relief. I said nothing, however, to him of my intention, but wrote the next morning to the committee of the Assembly, who had the disposition of some public money, warmly recommending the case of these officers to their consideration, and proposing that a present should be sent them of necessaries and refreshments. My son, who had some experience of a camp life and of its wants, drew up a list for me, which I inclosed in my letter. The committee approved, and used such diligence that, conducted by my son, the stores arrived at the camp as soon as the wagons. They consisted of twenty parcels, each containing

6 lbs. loaf sugar.	1 keg containing 20 lbs. good
6 do. Muscovado do.	butter.
1 lb. green tea.	2 dozen old Madeira wine.
1 do. bohea do.	2 gallons Jamaica spirits.
6 lbs. ground coffee.	1 bottle flour of mustard.
6 do. chocolate.	2 well-cured hams.
1/2 chest best white biscuit.	1/2 dozen dried tongues.
1/2 lb. pepper.	6 lbs. rice.
1 quart white vinegar.	6 do. raisins.
1 Gloucester cheese.	

These parcels, well packed, were placed on as many horses, each parcel, with the horse, being intended as a present for one officer. They were very thankfully received and the kindness acknowledged by letters to me, from the colonels of both regiments, in the most grateful terms. The general, too, was highly satisfied with my conduct in procuring him the wagons, and readily paid my account of disbursements, thanking me repeatedly and requesting my further assistance in sending provisions after him. I undertook this also, and was busily employed in it till we heard of his defeat; advancing for the service, of my own money, upward of one thousand pounds sterling, of which I sent him an account. It came to his hands, luckily for me, a few days before the battle, and he returned me immediately an order on the paymaster for the round sum of one thousand pounds, leaving the remainder to the next account. I consider this payment as good luck, having never been able to obtain the remainder; of which more hereafter.

This general was, I think, a brave man, and might probably have made a figure as a good officer in some European war. But he had too much self-confidence, too high an opinion of the validity of regular troops, and too mean a one of both Americans and Indians. George Croghan, our Indian interpreter, joined him on his march with one hundred of those people, who might have been of great use to his army as guides and scouts if he had treated them kindly; but he slighted and neglected them and they gradually left him.

In conversation with him one day, he was giving me some account of his intended progress. "After taking Fort Duquesne," said he, "I am to proceed to Niagara; and having taken that, to Frontenac, if the season will allow time, and I suppose it will; for Duquesne can hardly detain me above three or four days, and then I see nothing that can obstruct my march to Niagara." Having before revolved in my mind the long line his army must make in their march by a very narrow road, to be cut for them through the woods and bushes, and also what I had read of a former defeat of fifteen hundred French who invaded the Illinois country, I had conceived some doubts and some fears for the event of the campaign. But I ventured only to say: "To be sure, sir, if you arrive well before Duquesne with these fine troops, so well provided with artillery, the fort, though completely fortified and assisted with a very strong garrison, can probably make but a short resistance. The only danger I apprehend of obstruction to your march is from the ambuscades of the Indians, who by constant practice are dexterous in laying and executing them; and the slender line, near four miles long, which your army must make, may expose it to be attacked by surprise in its flanks and to be cut like a thread into several pieces, which from their distance cannot come up in time to support each other."

He smiled at my ignorance and replied: "These savages may indeed be a formidable enemy to your raw American militia, but upon the king's regular and disciplined troops, sir, it is impossible they should make any impression." I was conscious of an impropriety in my disputing with a military man in matters of his profession, and said no more. The enemy, however, did not take the advantage of his army which I apprehended its long line of march exposed it to, but let it advance without interruption till within nine miles of the place; and then, when more in a body (for it had just passed a river, where the front had halted till all were come over) and in a more open part of the woods than any it had passed, attacked its advance-guard by a heavy fire from behind trees and bushes, which was the first intelligence the general had of an enemy's being near him. This guard being disordered, the general hurried the troops up to their assistance, which was done in great confusion through wagons, baggage, and cattle, and presently the fire came upon their flank. The officers being on horseback were more easily distinguished, picked out as marks, and fell very fast; and the soldiers were crowded together in a huddle, having or hearing no orders and standing to be shot at till two-thirds of them were killed, and then, being seized with a panic, the remainder fled with precipitation.

The wagoners took each a horse out of his team and scampered. Their example was immediately followed by others, so that all the wagons, provisions, artillery, and stores were left to the enemy. The general being wounded was brought off with difficulty; his secretary, Mr. Shirley, was killed by his side, and out of eighty-six officers sixty-three were killed or wounded, and seven hundred and fourteen men killed of eleven hundred. These eleven hundred had been picked men from the whole army; the rest had been left behind with Colonel Dunbar, who was to follow with the heavier part of the stores, provisions, and baggage. The flyers, not being pursued, arrived at Dunbar's camp, and the panic they brought with them instantly seized him and all his people. And though he had now above one thousand men, and the enemy who had beaten Braddock did not at most exceed four hundred Indians and French together, instead of proceeding and endeavoring to recover some of the lost honor, he ordered all the stores, ammunition, etc., to be destroyed, that he might have more horses to assist his flight toward the settlements and less lumber to remove. He was there met with requests from the governors of Virginia, Maryland, and Pennsylvania that he would post his troops on the frontiers, so as to afford some protection to the inhabitants, but he continued his hasty march through all the country, not thinking himself safe till he arrived at Philadelphia, where the inhabitants could protect him. This whole transaction gave us Americans the first suspicion that our exalted ideas of the prowess of British regular troops had not been well founded.

In their first march, too, from their landing till they got beyond the settlements, they had plundered and stripped the inhabitants, totally ruining some poor families, besides insulting, abusing, and confining the people if they remonstrated. This was enough to put us out of conceit of such defenders if we had really wanted any. How different was the conduct of our French friends in 1781, who during a march through the most inhabited part of our country, from Rhode Island to Virginia, near seven hundred miles, occasioned not the smallest complaint for the loss of a pig, a chicken, or even an apple.

Captain Orme, who was one of the general's aids-de-camp, and being grievously wounded, was brought off with him and continued with him to his death, which happened in a few days, told me that he was totally silent all the first day, and at night only said: "Who would have thought it?" That he was silent again the following day, saying only at last, "We shall better know how to deal with them another time," and died in a few minutes after.

The secretary's papers, with all the general's orders, instructions, and correspondence, falling into the enemy's hands, they selected and translated into French a number of the articles, which they printed, to prove the hostile intentions of the British court before the declaration of war. Among these I saw some letters of the general to the ministry, speaking highly of the great service I had rendered to the army and recommending me to their notice. David Hume, who was some years afterward secretary to Lord Hertford when minister in France, and afterward to General Conway when Secretary of State, told he had seen among the papers in that office letters from Braddock highly recommending me. But the expedition having been unfortunate, my service, it seems, was not thought of much value, for those recommendations were never of any use to me.

As to rewards from himself, I asked only one, which was that he would give orders to his officers not to enlist any more of our bought servants and that he would discharge such as had been already enlisted. This he readily granted, and several were accordingly returned to their masters on my application. Dunbar, when the command devolved on him, was not so generous. He being at Philadelphia on his retreat, or rather flight, I applied to him for the discharge of the servants of three poor farmers of Lancaster County that he had enlisted, reminding him of the late general's orders on that head. He promised me that if the masters would come to him at Trenton, where he should be in a few days on his march to New York, he would there deliver their men to them. They accordingly were at the expense and trouble of going to Trenton, and there he refused to perform his promise, to their great loss and disappointment.

As soon as the loss of the wagons and horses was generally known, all the owners came upon me for the valuation which I had given bond to pay. Their demands gave me a great deal of trouble. I acquainted them that the money was ready in the paymaster's hands, but the order for paying it must first be obtained from General Shirley, and that I had applied for it, but he being at a distance an answer could not soon be received, and they must have patience. All this, however, was not sufficient to satisfy them, and some began to sue me. General Shirley at length relieved me from this terrible situation by appointing commissioners to examine the claims and ordering payment. They amounted to near twenty thousand pounds, which to pay would have ruined me.

Before we had the news of this defeat, the two Doctors Bond came to me with a subscription paper for raising money to defray the expenses of a grand firework, which it was intended to exhibit at a rejoicing on receiving the news of our taking Fort Duquesne. I looked grave and said it would, I thought, be time enough to prepare the rejoicing when we knew we should have occasion to rejoice. They seemed surprised that I did not immediately comply with their proposal. "Why the d—l!" said one of them; "You surely don't suppose that the fort will not be taken?" "I don't know that it will not be taken, but I know that the events of war are subject to great uncertainty." I gave them the reasons of my doubting; the subscription was dropped, and the projectors thereby missed the mortification they would have undergone if the firework had been prepared. Dr. Bond, on some other occasion afterward, said that he did not like Franklin's forebodings.

CHAPTER XI

GOVERNOR Morris, who had continually worried the Assembly with message after message before the defeat of Braddock, to beat them into the making of acts to raise money for the defense of the province without taxing among others the proprietary estates, and had rejected all their bills for not having such an exempting clause, now redoubled his attacks with more hope of success, the danger and necessity being greater. The Assembly, however, continued firm, believing they had justice on their side, and that it would be giving up an essential right if they suffered the governor to amend their money bills. In one of the last, indeed, which was for granting fifty thousand pounds, his proposed amendment was only of a single word. The bill expressed that "all estates real and personal were to be taxed; those of the proprietaries *not* excepted." His amendment was: for *not*, read *only*. A small but very material alteration. However, when the news of the disaster reached England, our friends there, whom we had taken care to furnish with all the Assembly's answers to the governor's messages, raised a clamor against the proprietaries for their meanness and injustice in giving their governor such instructions; some going so far as to say that by obstructing the defense of their province they forfeited their right to it. They were intimidated by this, and sent orders to their Receiver-General to add five thousand pounds of their money to whatever sum might be given by the Assembly for such purpose.

This being testified to the House was accepted in lieu of their share of a general tax; and a new bill was formed with an exempting clause, which passed accordingly. By this act I was appointed one of the commissioners for disposing of the money—sixty thousand pounds. I had been active in modeling the bill and procuring its passage, and had at the same time drawn one for establishing and disciplining a voluntary militia, which I carried through the House without much difficulty, as care was taken in it to leave the Quakers at liberty. To promote the association necessary to form the militia, I wrote a dialogue stating and answering all the objections I could think of to such a militia, which was printed, and had, as I thought, great effect.

While the several companies in the city and country were forming and learning their exercise, the governor prevailed with me to take charge of our northwestern frontier, which was infested by the enemy, and provide for the defense of the inhabitants by raising troops and building a line of forts. I undertook this military business, though I did not conceive myself well qualified for it. He gave me a commission with full powers and a parcel of blank commissions for officers, to be given to whom I thought fit. I had but little difficulty in raising men, having soon five hundred and sixty under my command. My son, who had in the preceding war been an officer in the army raised against Canada, was my aid-de-camp and of great use to me. The Indians had burned Gnadenhutten, a village settled by the Moravians, and massacred the inhabitants; but the place was thought a good situation for one of the forts.

In order to march thither, I assembled the companies at Bethlehem, the chief establishment of these people. I was surprised to find it in so good a posture of defense; the destruction of Gnadenhutten had made them apprehend danger. The principal buildings were defended by a stockade; they had purchased a quantity of arms and ammunition from New York, and had even placed quantities of small paving-stones between the windows of their high stone houses, for their women to throw them down upon the heads of any Indians that should attempt to force into them. The armed brethren, too, kept watch and relieved each other on guard as methodically as in any garrison town. In conversation with the bishop, Spangenberg, I mentioned my surprise; for, knowing they had obtained an act of Parliament exempting them from military duties in the colonies, I had supposed they were conscientiously scrupulous of bearing arms. He answered me that it was not one of their established principles; but at the time of their obtaining that act it was thought to be a principle with many of their people. On this occasion, however, they, to their surprise, found it adopted by but few. It seemed they were either deceived in themselves or deceived the Parliament; but common sense, aided by present danger, will sometimes be too strong for whimsical opinions.

It was the beginning of January when we set out upon this business of building forts. I sent one detachment toward the Minisink, with instructions to erect one for the security of that upper part of the country; and another to the lower part, with similar instructions; and I concluded to go myself with the rest of my force to Gnadenhutten, where a fort was thought more immediately necessary. The Moravians procured me five wagons for our tools, stores, and baggage.

Just before we had left Bethlehem, eleven farmers, who had been driven from their plantations by the Indians, came to me requesting a supply of fire-arms, that they might go back and bring off their cattle. I gave them each a gun with suitable ammunition. We had not marched many miles before it began to rain, and it continued raining all day; there were no habitations on the road to shelter us till we arrived near night at the house of a German, where, and in his barn, we were all huddled together, as wet as water could make us. It was well we were not attacked in our march, for our arms were of the most ordinary sort, and our men could not keep the locks of their guns dry. The Indians are dexterous in contrivances for that purpose, which we had not. They met that day the eleven poor farmers above mentioned, and killed ten of them. The one that escaped informed us that his and his companions' guns would not go off, the priming being wet with the rain.

The next day being fair we continued our march, and arrived at the desolated Gnadenhutten. There was a mill near, round which were left several pine boards, with which we soon hutted ourselves; an operation the more necessary at that inclement season, as we had no tents. Our first work was to bury more effectually the dead we found there, who had been half-interred by the country people.

The next morning our fort was planned and marked out, the circumference measuring four hundred and fifty-five feet, which would require as many palisades to be made, one with another, of a foot diameter each. Our axes, of which we had seventy, were immediately set to work to cut down trees, and our men being dexterous in the use of them, great dispatch was made. Seeing the trees fall so fast, I had the curiosity to look at my watch when two men began to cut at a pine; in six minutes they had it upon the ground, and I found it of fourteen inches diameter. Each pine made three palisades of eighteen feet long, pointed at one end. While these were preparing, our other men dug a trench all round, of three feet deep, in which the palisades were to be planted; and the bodies being taken off our wagons and the fore and hind wheels separated by taking out the pin which united the two parts of the perch, we had ten carriages, with two horses each, to bring the palisades from the woods to the spot. When they were set up our carpenters built a platform of boards all round within, about six feet high, for the men to stand on when to fire through the loop-holes. We had one swivel gun, which we mounted on one of the angles, and fired it as soon as fixed, to let the Indians know, if any were within hearing, that we had such pieces; and thus our fort, if that name may be given to so miserable a stockade, was finished in a week, though it rained so hard every other day that the men could not work.

This gave me occasion to observe that when men are employed they are best contented; for on the days they worked they were good-natured and cheerful, and with the consciousness of having done a good day's work they spent the evening jollily; but on our idle days they were mutinous and quarrelsome, finding fault with the pork, the bread, etc., and were continually in bad humor, which put me in mind of a sea-captain whose rule it was to keep his men constantly at work; and when his mate once told him that they had done everything and there was nothing further to employ them about, "Oh," said he, "make them scour the anchor."

This kind of fort, however contemptible, is a sufficient defense against Indians, who have no cannon. Finding ourselves now posted securely and having a place to retreat to on occasion, we ventured out in parties to scour the adjacent country. We met with no Indians, but we found the places on the neighboring hills where they had lain to watch our proceedings. There was an art in their contrivance of those places that seems worth mentioning. It being winter, a fire was necessary for them; but a common fire on the surface of the ground would, by its light, have discovered their position at a distance. They had, therefore, dug holes in the ground about three feet in diameter and somewhat deeper; we found where they had, with their hatchets, cut off the charcoal from the sides of burnt logs lying in the woods. With these coals they had made small fires in the bottom of the holes, and we observed among the weeds and grass the prints of their bodies, made by their lying all round with their legs hanging down in the holes to keep their feet warm, which, with them, is an essential point. This kind of fire so managed could not discover them, either by its light, flame, sparks, or even smoke. It appeared that the number was not great, and it seems they saw we were too many to be attacked by them with prospect of advantage.

We had for our chaplain a zealous Presbyterian minister, Mr. Beatty, who complained to me that the men did not generally attend his prayers and exhortations. When they enlisted they were promised, besides pay and provisions, a gill of rum a day, which was punctually served out to them, half in the morning and the other half in the evening, and I observed they were punctual in attending to receive it; upon which I said to Mr. Beatty: "It is perhaps below the dignity of your profession to act as steward of the rum, but if you were only to distribute it out after prayers you would have them all about you." He liked the thought, undertook the task, and with the help of a few hands to measure out the liquor executed it to satisfaction, and never were prayers more generally and more punctually attended. So that I think this method preferable to the punishment inflicted by some military laws for non-attendance on divine service.

I had hardly finished this business and got my fort well stored with provisions when I received a letter from the governor, acquainting me that he had called the Assembly, and wished my attendance there if the posture of affairs on the frontiers was such that my remaining there was no longer necessary. My friends, too, of the Assembly, pressing me by their letters to be, if possible, at the meeting, and my three intended forts being now completed and the inhabitants contented to remain on their farms under that protection, I resolved to return, the more willingly as a New England officer, Colonel Clapham, experienced in Indian war, being on a visit to our establishment, consented to accept the command. I gave him a commission, and parading the garrison had it read before them and introduced him to them as an officer who, from his skill in military affairs, was much more fit to command them than myself, and giving them a little exhortation, took my leave. I was escorted as far as Bethlehem, where I rested a few days to recover from the fatigue I had undergone. The first night, lying in a good bed, I could hardly sleep, it was so different from my hard lodging on the floor of a hut at Gnadenhutten with only a blanket or two.

While at Bethlehem I inquired a little into the practices of the Moravians; some of them had accompanied me, and all were very kind to me. I found they worked for a common stock, ate at common tables, and slept in common dormitories, great numbers together. In the dormitories I observed loop-holes at certain distances all along just under the ceiling, which I thought judiciously placed for change of air. I went to their church, where I was entertained with good music, the organ being accompanied with violins, hautboys, flutes, clarinets, etc. I understood their sermons were not usually preached to mixed congregations of men, women, and children, as is our common practice, but that they assembled, sometimes the married men, at other times their wives, then the young men, the young women, and the little children; each division by itself. The sermon I heard was to the latter, who came in and were placed in rows on benches; the boys under the conduct of a young man, their tutor, and the girls conducted by a young woman. The discourse seemed well adapted to their capacities, and was delivered in a pleasing, familiar manner, coaxing them, as it were, to be good. They behaved very orderly, but looked pale and unhealthy, which made me suspect they were kept too much within doors or not allowed sufficient exercise.

I inquired concerning the Moravian marriages, whether the report was true that they were by lot. I was told that lots were used only in particular cases; that generally when a young man found himself disposed to marry he informed the elders of his class, who consulted the elder ladies that governed the young women. As these elders of the different sexes were well acquainted with the tempers and dispositions of their respective pupils, they could best judge what matches were suitable, and their judgments were generally acquiesced in. But if, for example, it should happen that two or three young women were found to be equally proper for the young man, the lot was then recurred to. I objected if the matches are not made by the mutual choice of the parties, some of them may chance to be very unhappy. "And so they may," answered my informer, "if you let the parties choose for themselves." Which indeed I could not deny.

Being returned to Philadelphia, I found the association went on with great success. The inhabitants that were not Quakers having pretty generally come into it formed themselves into companies, and chose their captains, lieutenants, and ensigns, according to the new law. Dr. Bond visited me and gave me an account of the pains he had taken to spread a general good liking of the law, and ascribed much to those endeavors. I had the vanity to ascribe all to my "Dialogue;" however, not knowing but that he might be in the right, I let him enjoy his opinion, which I take to be generally the best way in such cases. The officers, meeting, chose me to be colonel of the regiment, which I this time accepted. I forget how many companies we had, but we paraded about twelve hundred well-looking men, with a company of artillery, who had been furnished with six brass field-pieces, which they had become so expert in the use of as to fire twelve times in a minute. The first time I reviewed my regiment they accompanied me to my house, and would salute me with some rounds fired before my door, which shook down and broke several glasses of my electrical apparatus. And my new honor proved not much less brittle; for all our commissions were soon after broken by a repeal of the law in England.

During this short time of my colonelship, being about to set out on a journey to Virginia, the officers of my regiment took it into their heads that it would be proper for them to escort me out of town as far as the Lower Ferry. Just as I was getting on horseback they came to my door, between thirty and forty, mounted, and all in their uniforms. I had not been previously acquainted with their project, or I should have prevented it, being naturally averse to the assuming of state on any occasion; and I was a good deal chagrined at their appearance, as I could not avoid their accompanying me. What made it worse was that as soon as we began to move they drew their swords and rode with them naked all the way. Somebody wrote an account of this to the proprietor, and it gave him great offense. No such honor had been paid to him when in the province nor to any of his governors, and he said it was only proper to princes of the blood royal; which may be true for aught I know, who was, and still am, ignorant of the etiquette in such cases.

This silly affair, however, greatly increased his rancor against me, which was before considerable on account of my conduct in the Assembly respecting the exemption of his estate from taxation, which I had always opposed very warmly, and not without severe reflections on the meanness and injustice of contending for it. He accused me to the ministry as being the great obstacle to the king's service, preventing by my influence in the House the proper form of the bills for raising money; and he instanced the parade with my officers as a proof of my having an intention to take the government of the province out of his hands by force. He also applied to Sir Everard Fawkener, the Postmaster-General, to deprive me of my office. But it had no other effect than to procure from Sir Everard a gentle admonition.

Notwithstanding the continual wrangle between the governor and the House, in which I as a member had so large a share, there still subsisted a civil intercourse between that gentleman and myself, and we never had any personal difference. I have sometimes since thought that his little or no resentment against me for the answers it was known I drew up to his messages might be the effect of professional habit, and that, being bred a lawyer, he might consider us both as merely advocates for contending clients in a suit; he for the proprietaries and I for the Assembly. He would, therefore, sometimes call in a friendly way to advise with me on difficult points, and sometimes, though not often, take my advice.

We acted in concert to supply Braddock's army with provisions, and when the shocking news arrived of his defeat the governor sent in haste for me, to consult with him on measures for preventing the desertion of the back counties. I forgot now the advice I gave; but I think it was that Dunbar should be written to and prevailed with, if possible, to post his troops on the frontiers for their protection, until by reëforcements from the colonies he might be able to proceed in the expedition. And after my return from the frontier he would have had me undertake the conduct of such an expedition with provincial troops for the reduction of Fort Duquesne, Dunbar and his men being otherwise employed; and he proposed to commission me as general. I had not so good an opinion of my military abilities as he professed to have, and I believe his professions must have exceeded his real sentiments; but probably he might think that my popularity would facilitate the business with the men and influence in the Assembly the grant of money to pay for it, and that, perhaps, without taxing the proprietary. Finding me not so forward to engage as he expected, the project was dropped, and he soon after left the government, being superseded by Captain Denny.

Before I proceed in relating the part I had in public affairs under this new governor's administration, it may not be amiss to give here some account of the rise and progress of my philosophical reputation.

In 1746, being in Boston, I met there with a Dr. Spence, who was lately arrived from Scotland and showed me some electric experiments. They were imperfectly performed, as he was not very expert; but being in a subject quite new to me, they equally surprised and pleased me. Soon after my return to Philadelphia our library company received from Mr. Peter Collinson, Fellow of the Royal Society of London, a present of a glass tube, with some account of the use of it in making such experiments. I eagerly seized the opportunity of repeating what I had seen at Boston, and by much practice acquired great readiness in performing those also which we had an account of from England, adding a number of new ones. I say much practice, for my house was continually full for some time with persons who came to see these new wonders.

To divide a little this incumbrance among my friends I caused a number of similar tubes to be blown in our glass-house, with which they furnished themselves, so that we had at length several performers. Among these the principal was Mr. Kinnersley, an ingenious neighbor, who, being out of business, I encouraged him to undertake showing the experiments for money, and drew up for him two lectures, in which the experiments were ranged in such order and accompanied with explanations in such method as that the foregoing should assist in comprehending the following. He procured an elegant apparatus for the purpose, in which all the little machines that I had roughly made for myself were neatly formed by instrument makers. His lectures were well attended and gave great satisfaction; and after some time he went through the colonies, exhibiting them in every capital town, and picked up some money. In the West India Islands, indeed, it was with difficulty the experiments could be made, from the general moisture of the air.

Obliged as we were to Mr. Collinson for the present of the tube, etc., I thought it right he should be informed of our success in using it, and wrote him several letters containing accounts of our experiments. He got them read in the Royal Society, where they were not at first thought worth so much notice as to be printed in their *Transactions*. One paper which I wrote for Mr. Kinnersley, on the sameness of lightning with electricity, I sent to Mr. Mitchel, an acquaintance of mine and one of the members also of that society, who wrote me word that it had been read, but was laughed at by the connoisseurs. The papers, however, being shown to Dr. Fothergill, he thought them of too much value to be stifled and advised the printing of them. Mr. Collinson then gave them to Cave for publication in his *Gentleman's Magazine,* but he chose to print them separately in a pamphlet, and Dr. Fothergill wrote the preface. Cave, it seems, judged rightly for his profession, for by the additions that arrived afterward they swelled to a quarto volume, which has had five editions and cost him nothing for copy-money.

It was, however, some time before those papers were much taken notice of in England. A copy of them happening to fall into the hands of the Count de Buffon, a philosopher, deservedly of great reputation in France and indeed all over Europe, he prevailed with M. Dubourg to translate them into French, and they were printed at Paris. The publication offended the Abbé Nollet, preceptor in natural philosophy to the royal family and an able experimenter, who had formed and published a theory of electricity, which then had the general vogue. He could not at first believe that such a work came from America, and said it must have been fabricated by his enemies at Paris to oppose his system. Afterward, having been assured that there really existed such a person as Franklin at Philadelphia, which he had doubted, he wrote and published a volume of letters, chiefly addressed to me, defending his theory and denying the verity of my experiments and of the positions deduced from them.

I once purposed answering the abbé and actually began the answer; but on consideration that my writings contained a description of experiments which any one might repeat and verify, and, if not to be verified, could not be defended, or of observations offered as *conjectures* and not delivered dogmatically, therefore not laying me under any obligation to defend them, and reflecting that a dispute between two persons, written in different languages, might be lengthened greatly by mistranslations, and thence misconceptions of one another's meaning, much of one of the abbé's letters being founded on an error in the translation, I concluded to let my papers shift for themselves, believing it was better to spend what time I could spare from public business in making new experiments than in disputing about those already made. I, therefore, never answered M. Nollet, and the event gave me no cause to repent my silence; for my friend, M. Le Roy, of the Royal Academy of Sciences, took up my cause and refuted him; my book was translated into the Italian, German, and Latin languages, and the doctrine it contained was by degrees generally adopted by the philosophers of Europe in preference to that of the abbé, so that he lived to see himself the last of his sect except M. B——, of Paris, his *élève* and immediate disciple.

What gave my book the more sudden and general celebrity was the success of one of its proposed experiments, made by MM. Dalibard and De Lor at Marley, for drawing lightning from the clouds. This engaged the public attention everywhere. M. De Lor, who had an apparatus for experimental philosophy and lectured in that branch of science, undertook to repeat what he called the Philadelphia experiments; and after they were performed before the king and court, all the curious of Paris flocked to see them. I will not swell this narrative with an account of that capital experiment, nor of the infinite pleasure I received in the success of a similar one I made soon after with a kite at Philadelphia, as both are to be found in the histories of electricity.

Dr. Wright, an English physician, when at Paris wrote to a friend, who was one of the Royal Society, an account of the high esteem my experiments were in among the learned abroad, and of their wonder that my writings had been so little noticed in England. The society on this resumed the consideration of the letters that had been read to them, and the celebrated Dr. Watson drew up a summary account of them and of all I had afterward sent to England on the subject, which he accompanied with some praise of the writer. This summary was then printed in their *Transactions;* and some members of the society in London, particularly the very ingenious Mr. Canton, having verified the experiment of procuring lightning from the clouds by a pointed rod and acquainted them with the success, they soon made me more than amends for the slight with which they had before treated me. Without my having made any application for that honor they chose me a member, and voted that I should be excused the customary payments, which would have amounted to twenty-five guineas; and ever since have given me their *Transactions* gratis.[1] They also presented me with the gold medal of Sir Godfrey Copley for the year 1753, the delivery of which was accompanied by a very handsome speech of the president, Lord Macclesfield, wherein I was highly honored.

CHAPTER XII

OUR new governor, Captain Denny, brought over for me the before-mentioned medal from the Royal Society, which he presented to me at an entertainment given him by the city. He accompanied it with very polite expressions of his esteem for me, having, as he said, been long acquainted with my character. After dinner, when the company, as was customary at that time, were engaged in drinking, he took me aside in another room, and acquainted me that he had been advised by his friends in England to cultivate a friendship with me, as one who was capable of giving him the best advice and of contributing most effectually to the making his administration easy. That he, therefore, desired of all things to have a good understanding with me, and he begged me to be assured of his readiness on all occasions to render me every service that might be in his power. He said much to me also of the proprietor's good disposition toward the province, and of the advantage it would be to us all, and to me in particular, if the opposition that had been so long continued to his measures were dropped and harmony restored between him and the people, in effecting which it was thought no one could be more serviceable than myself; and I might depend on adequate acknowledgments and recompenses. The drinkers, finding we did not return immediately to the table, sent us a decanter of Madeira, which the governor made a liberal use of, and in proportion became more profuse of his solicitations and promises.

My answers were to this purpose: that my circumstances, thanks to God, were such as to make proprietary favors unnecessary to me; and that, being a member of the Assembly, I could not possibly accept of any; that, however, I had no personal enmity to the proprietary, and that whenever the public measures he proposed should appear to be for the good of the people, no one would espouse and forward them more zealously than myself; my past opposition having been founded on this, that the measures which had been urged were evidently intended to serve the proprietary interest, with great prejudice to that of the people. That I was much obliged to him (the governor) for his profession of regard to me, and he might rely on everything in my power to render his administration as easy to him as possible, hoping at the same time that he had not brought with him the same unfortunate instructions his predecessors had been hampered with.

On this he did not then explain himself; but when he afterward came to do business with the Assembly they appeared again, the disputes were renewed, and I was as active as ever in the opposition, being the penman, first of the request to have a communication of the instructions, and then of the remarks upon them, which may be found in the votes of the times and in the *Historical Review* I afterward published. But between us personally no enmity arose; we were often together; he was a man of letters, had seen much of the world, and was entertaining and pleasing in conversation. He gave me information that my old friend Ralph was still alive; that he was esteemed one of the best political writers in England; had been employed in the dispute between Prince Frederick and the king, and had obtained a pension of three hundred pounds a year; that his reputation was indeed small as a poet, Pope having damned his poetry in the *Dunciad;* but his prose was thought as good as any man's.

The Assembly finally finding the proprietary obstinately persisted in shackling the deputies with instructions inconsistent, not only with the privileges of the people, but with the service of the crown, resolved to petition the king against them, and appointed me their agent to go over to England to present and support the petition. The House had sent up a bill to the governor, granting a sum of sixty thousand pounds for the king's use (ten thousand pounds of which was subjected to the orders of the then general, Lord Loudoun), which the governor, in compliance with his instructions, absolutely refused to pass.

I had agreed with Captain Morris, of the packet at New York, for my passage, and my stores were put on board, when Lord Loudoun arrived at Philadelphia, expressly, as he told me, to endeavor an accommodation between the governor and Assembly, that his majesty's service might not be obstructed by their dissensions. Accordingly he desired the governor and myself to meet him, that he might hear what was to be said on both sides. We met and discussed the business. In behalf of the Assembly I urged the various arguments that may be found in the public papers of that time, which were of my writing and are printed with the minutes of the Assembly; and the governor pleaded his instructions, the bond he had given to observe them, and his ruin if he disobeyed, yet seemed not unwilling to hazard himself if Lord Loudoun would advise it. This his lordship did not choose to do, though I once thought I had nearly prevailed with him to do it; but finally he rather chose to urge the compliance of the Assembly; and he entreated me to use my endeavors with them for that purpose, declaring that he would spare none of the king's troops for the defense of our frontiers, and that if we did not continue to provide for that defense ourselves they must remain exposed to the enemy.

I acquainted the House with what had passed, and presenting them with a set of resolutions I had drawn up declaring our rights, that we did not relinquish our claim to those rights, but only suspended the exercise of them on this occasion through *force*, against which we protested, they at length agreed to drop that bill and frame another conformable to the proprietary instructions. This, of course, the governor passed, and I was then at liberty to proceed on my voyage; but in the mean time the packet had sailed with my sea-stores, which was some loss to me, and my only recompense was his lordship's thanks for my service, all the credit of obtaining the accommodation falling to his share.

He set out for New York before me, and as the time for dispatching the packet-boats was at his disposition and there were two then remaining there, one of which, he said, was to sail very soon, I requested to know the precise time, that I might not miss her by any delay of mine. The answer was: "I have given out that she is to sail on Saturday next, but I may let you know, *entre nous,* that if you are there by Monday morning you will be in time, but do not delay longer." By some accidental hindrance at a ferry it was Monday noon before I arrived, and I was much afraid she might have sailed, as the wind was fair; but I was soon made easy by the information that she was still in the harbor, and would not move till the next day. One would imagine that I was now on the very point of departing for Europe. I thought so; but I was not then so well acquainted with his lordship's character, of which *indecision* was one of his strongest features. I shall give some instances. It was about the beginning of April that I came to New York, and I think it was near the end of June before we sailed. There were then two of the packet-boats, which had been long in readiness, but were detained for the general's letters, which were always to be ready *to-morrow.* Another packet arrived. She, too, was detained, and before we sailed a fourth was expected. Ours was the first to be dispatched as having been there the longest. Passengers were engaged for all, and some extremely impatient to be gone and the merchants uneasy about their letters, and for the orders they had given for insurance (it being war-time) and for autumnal goods; but their anxiety availed nothing. His lordship's letters were not ready, and yet whoever waited on him found him always at his desk, pen in hand, and concluded he must needs write abundantly.

Going myself one morning to pay my respects, I found in his antechamber one Innis, a messenger of Philadelphia, who had come thence express, with a packet from Governor Denny for the general. He delivered to me some letters from my friends there, which occasioned my inquiring when he was to return and where he lodged, that I might send some letters by him. He told me he was ordered to call to-morrow at nine for the general's answer to the governor, and should set off immediately. I put my letters into his hands the same day. A fortnight after I met him again in the same place. "So you are soon returned, Innis?" "Returned! no, I am not gone yet." "How so?" "I have called here this and every morning these two weeks past for his lordship's letters, and they are not yet ready." "Is it possible, when he is so great a writer? for I see him constantly at his escritoire." "Yes," said Innis, "but he is like St. George on the signs, *always on horseback and never rides on.*" This observation of the messenger was, it seems, well founded; for when in England I understood that Mr. Pitt, afterward Lord Chatham, gave it as one reason for removing this general and sending Generals Amherst and Wolfe, *that the minister never heard from him and could not know what he was doing.*

In this daily expectation of sailing, and all the three packets going down to Sandy Hook to join the fleet there, the passengers thought it best to be on board, lest by a sudden order the ships should sail and they be left behind. There, if I remember, we were about six weeks, consuming our sea-stores and obliged to procure more. At length the fleet sailed, the general and all his army on board, bound to Louisbourg, with intent to besiege and take that fortress; and all the packet-boats in company were ordered to attend the general's ship, ready to receive his dispatches when they should be ready. We were out five days before we got a letter with leave to part, and then our ship quitted the fleet and steered for England. The other two packets he still detained, carried them with him to Halifax, where he stayed some time to exercise the men in sham attacks upon sham forts, then altered his mind as to besieging Louisbourg and returned to New York with all his troops, together with the two packets above mentioned and all their passengers! During his absence the French and savages had taken Fort George, on the frontier of that province, and the Indians had massacred many of the garrison after capitulation.

On the whole, I wondered much how such a man came to be intrusted with so important a business as the conduct of a great army; but having since seen more of the great world and the means of obtaining and motives for giving places and employments, my wonder is diminished. General Shirley, on whom the command of the army devolved upon the death of Braddock, would, in my opinion, if continued in place have made a much better campaign than that of Loudoun in 1756, which was frivolous, expensive, and disgraceful to our nation beyond conception. For though Shirley was not bred a soldier, he was sensible and sagacious in himself and attentive to good advice from others, capable of forming judicious plans and quick and active in carrying them into execution. Loudoun, instead of defending the colonies with his great army, left them totally exposed while he paraded idly at Halifax, by which means Fort George was lost; besides, he deranged all our mercantile operations and distressed our trade by a long embargo on the exportation of provisions, on pretense of keeping supplies from being obtained by the enemy, but in reality for beating down their price in favor of the contractors, in whose profits it was said, perhaps from suspicion only, he had a share; and when at length the embargo was taken off, neglecting to send notice of it to Charleston, where the Carolina fleet was detained near three months, and whereby their bottoms were so much damaged by the worm that a great part of them foundered in their passage home.

Shirley was, I believe, sincerely glad of being relieved from so burdensome a charge as the conduct of an army must be to a man unacquainted with military business. I was at the entertainment given by the city of New York to Lord Loudoun on his taking upon him the command. Shirley, though thereby superseded, was present also. There was a great company of officers, citizens, and strangers, and some chairs having been borrowed in the neighborhood, there was one among them very low, which fell to the lot of Mr. Shirley. I sat by him, and perceiving it I said: "They have given you a very low seat." "No matter, Mr. Franklin," said he; "I find *a low seat* the easiest."

While I was, as before mentioned, detained at New York, I received all the accounts of the provisions, etc., that I had furnished to Braddock, some of which accounts could not sooner be obtained from the different persons I had employed to assist in the business. I presented them to Lord Loudoun, desiring to be paid the balance. He caused them to be examined by the proper officer, who, after comparing every article with its voucher, certified them to be right; and his lordship promised to give me an order on the paymaster for the balance due to me. This was, however, put off from time to time, and though I called often for it by appointment, I did not get it. At length, just before my departure, he told me he had, on better consideration, concluded not to mix his accounts with those of his predecessors. "And you," said he, "when in England, have only to exhibit your accounts to the Treasury and you will be paid immediately."

I mentioned, but without effect, a great and unexpected expense I had been put to by being detained so long at New York as a reason for my desiring to be presently paid, and on my observing that it was not right I should be put to any further trouble or delay in obtaining the money I had advanced, as I charged no commission for my service, "Oh," said he, "you must not think of persuading us that you are no gainer; we understand better those matters and know that every one concerned in supplying the army finds means, in the doing it, to fill his own pockets." I assured him that was not my case and that I had not pocketed a farthing; but he appeared clearly not to believe me, and indeed, I afterward learned that immense fortunes are often made in such employments. As to my balance, I am not paid it to this day; of which more hereafter.

Our captain of the packet boasted much, before we sailed, of the swiftness of his ship; unfortunately, when we came to sea she proved the dullest of ninety-six sail, to his no small mortification. After many conjectures respecting the cause, when we were near another ship, almost as dull as ours, which, however, gained upon us, the captain ordered all hands to come aft and stand as near the ensign staff as possible. We were, passengers included, about forty persons. While we stood there the ship mended her pace and soon left her neighbor far behind, which proved clearly what our captain suspected — that she was loaded too much by the head. The casks of water, it seems, had been all placed forward; these he therefore ordered to be moved further aft, on which the ship recovered her character and proved the best sailer in the fleet.

The captain said she had once gone at the rate of thirteen knots, which is accounted thirteen miles per hour. We had on board as a passenger Captain Archibald Kennedy, of the Royal Navy, who contended that it was impossible; that no ship ever sailed so fast, and that there must have been some error in the division of the log-line or some mistake in heaving the log. A wager ensued between the two captains, to be decided when there should be sufficient wind. Kennedy therefore examined the log-line, and being satisfied with it he determined to throw the log himself. Some days after, when the wind was very fair and fresh, and the captain of the packet, Lutwidge, said he believed she then went at the rate of thirteen knots, Kennedy made the experiment and owned his wager lost.

The foregoing fact I give for the sake of the following observation. It has been remarked as an imperfection in the art of ship-building that it can never be known till she is tried whether a new ship will or will not be a good sailer; for that the model of a good sailing-ship has been exactly followed in a new one, which has been proved on the contrary remarkably dull. I apprehend that this may partly be occasioned by the different opinions of seamen respecting the modes of loading, rigging, and sailing of a ship. Each has his method; and the same vessel, laden by the method and orders of one captain, shall sail worse than when by the orders of another. Besides, it scarce ever happens that a ship is formed, fitted for the sea, and sailed by the same person. One man builds the hull, another rigs her, a third loads and sails her. No one of these has the advantage of knowing all the ideas and experience of the others, and therefore cannot draw just conclusions from a combination of the whole.

Even in the simple operation of sailing, when at sea I have often observed different judgments in the officers who commanded the successive watches, the wind being the same. One would have the sails trimmed sharper or flatter than another, so that they seemed to have no certain rules to govern by. Yet I think a set of experiments might be instituted, first, to determine the most proper form of the hull for swift sailing; next, the best dimensions and most proper place for the masts; then the form and quantity of sails and their position, as the winds may be; and lastly, the disposition of the lading. This is an age of experiments, and I think a set accurately made and combined would be of great use.

We were several times chased in our passage, but outsailed everything, and in thirty days had soundings. We had a good observation, and the captain judged himself so near our port, Falmouth, that if we made a good run in the night we might be off the mouth of that harbor in the morning; and by running in the night might escape the notice of the enemy's privateers, who often cruised near the entrance of the Channel. Accordingly all the sail was set that we could possibly carry, and the wind being very fresh and fair, we stood right before it and made great way. The captain, after his observation, shaped his course, as he thought, so as to pass wide of the Scilly Rocks; but it seems there is sometimes a strong current setting up St. George's Channel, which formerly caused the loss of Sir Cloudesley Shovel's squadron in 1707. This was probably also the cause of what happened to us.

We had a watchman placed in the bow, to whom they often called, *"Look well out before there,"* and he as often answered *"Ay, ay;"* but perhaps had his eyes shut and was half-asleep at the time, they sometimes answering, as is said, mechanically; for he did not see a light just before us, which had been hid by the studding-sails from the man at the helm and from the rest of the watch, but by an accidental yaw of the ship was discovered and occasioned a great alarm, we being very near it; the light appearing to me as large as a cart-wheel. It was midnight and our captain fast asleep; but Captain Kennedy, jumping upon deck and seeing the danger, ordered the ship to veer round, all sails standing; an operation dangerous to the masts, but it carried us clear and we avoided shipwreck, for we were running fast on the rocks, on which the light was erected. This deliverance impressed me strongly with the utility of light-houses, and made me resolve to encourage the building some of them in America if I should live to return thither.

In the morning it was found by the soundings that we were near our port, but a thick fog hid the land from our sight. About nine o'clock the fog began to rise, and seemed to be lifted up from the water like a curtain of a theater, discovering underneath the town of Falmouth, the vessels in the harbor, and the fields that surround it. This was a pleasing spectacle to those who had been long without any other prospect than the uniform view of a vacant ocean, and it gave us the more pleasure, as we were now free from the anxieties which had arisen.[1]

I set out immediately with my son for London, and we only stopped a little by the way to view Stonehenge on Salisbury Plain, and Lord Pembroke's house and gardens, with the very curious antiquities, at Wilton. We arrived in London the 27th of July, 1757.

ENDNOTES

CHAPTER I

[1] In the Island of Nantucket.

[2] Commonly called "chap-books," a term applied to popular storybooks which in former days used to be hawked about by chap-men; such as "Tom Hickathrift," "Jack the Giant Killer," etc. Burton's histories were of rather a better class and comprised "The English Hero; or, Sir Francis Drake Revived;" "Admirable Curiosities," etc., etc.

CHAPTER III

[1] A comedian of eminence.

[2] A printing-house is called a *chapel* by the workmen.

CHAPTER IV

[1] This *plan* does not exist in the manuscript journal found among Dr. Franklin's papers, which appears, by a note thereon to be a *"copy made at Reading, in Pennsylvania, October 2d, 1787."*

[2] Dr. Franklin, in a letter to Benjamin Vaughan, dated November 9th, 1779, gives a further account of this pamphlet in these words:

"It was addressed to Mr. J. R., that is, James Ralph, then a youth of about my age and my intimate friend, afterward a political writer and historian. The purport of it was to prove the doctrine of fate, from the supposed attributes of God, in some such manner as this. That in erecting and governing the world, as he was infinitely wise he knew what would be best; infinitely good, he must be disposed; and infinitely powerful, he must be able to execute it. Consequently *all is right.*

"There were only a hundred copies printed, of which I gave a few to friends; and afterward disliking the piece, as conceiving it might have an ill tendency, I burned the rest, except one copy, the margin of which was filled with manuscript notes by Lyons, author of 'The Infallibility of Human Judgment,' who was at the time another of my acquaintance in London. I was not nineteen years of age when it was written. In 1730 I wrote a piece on the other side of the question, which began with laying for its foundation this fact: *'That almost all men in all ages and countries have at times made use of* PRAYER.' Thence I reasoned that if all things are ordained, prayer must among the rest be ordained. But as prayer can procure no change in things that are ordained, prayer must then be useless and an absurdity. God would therefore not ordain praying if everything else was ordained. But praying exists, therefore all other things are not ordained, etc. This pamphlet was never printed and the manuscript has long been lost. The great uncertainty I found in metaphysical reasonings disgusted me, and I quitted that kind of reading and study for others more satisfactory."

CHAPTER V

[1] Godfrey's claims to this invention are fully explained and confirmed in Miller's "Retrospect of the Eighteenth Century," Vol. I., pp. 468–480.

[2] It was called the *Pennsylvania Gazette*. Franklin and Meredith began the paper with No. 40, September 25th, 1729.

[3] The dissolution of the partnership was a year later, as appears by the following agreement, transcribed from the original in Franklin's handwriting. — ED.

"Be it remembered, that Hugh Meredith and Benjamin Franklin have this day separated as partners, and will henceforth act each on his own account; and that the said Hugh Meredith, for a valuable consideration by him received from the said Benjamin Franklin, hath relinquished, and doth hereby relinquish, to the said Franklin, all claim, right, or property to or in the printing materials and stock heretofore jointly possessed by them in partnership; and to all debts due to them as partners in the course of their business; which are all from henceforth the sole property of the said Benjamin Franklin. In witness whereof, I have hereunto set my hand this 14th day of July, 1730. HUGH MEREDITH."

[4] "It is little known or set down to the condemnation of Franklin that, when he was young in business, and stood in need of sundry articles in the line of his profession as a printer, he had the ingenuity to make them for himself. In this way he founded letters of lead, engraved various printing ornaments, cut wood-cuts, made printer's ink, engraved copper-plate vignettes, and made his plate-press." — Watson's "Annals of Philadelphia," p. 513.

Mr. Watson relates another anecdote. He says that the "yellow willow tree," now so common throughout the country, was first introduced into America by Franklin. A wicker-basket made of willow, in which some foreign article had been imported, he saw sprouting in a ditch, and directed some of the twigs to be planted. They took root, and from these shoots are supposed to have sprung all the yellow willows which have grown on this side of the Atlantic.

Chaptal ascribes to Franklin also the introduction of the agricultural use of plaster of Paris into the United States. "As this celebrated philosopher," says he, "wished that the effects of this manure should strike the gaze of all cultivators, he wrote in great letters, formed by the use of the ground plaster, in a field of clover lying upon the great road, *'This has been plastered.'* The prodigious vegetation which was developed in the plastered portion led him to adopt this method. Volumes upon the excellency of plaster would not have produced so speedy a revolution. From that period the Americans have imported great quantities of plaster of Paris."—Chaptal's "Agricultural Chemistry," Boston edition, p. 73.—ED.

CHAPTER VI

[1] Down to this period the memoir was written in the year 1771, and the task was then laid aside for several years. In the mean time the manuscript was shown to several of the author's friends, who pressed him to complete what he had begun. He accordingly yielded to their solicitations, and to the part with which this chapter commences he prefixed the following introductory remarks and also the two letters to which he alludes.

[2] This little book is dated *Sunday, 1st July, 1733.*—W. T. F.

CHAPTER VIII

[1] In the early part of his life Mr. Whitefield was preaching in an open field, when a drummer happened to be present who was determined to interrupt his pious business, and rudely beat his drum in a violent manner in order to drown the preacher's voice. Mr. Whitefield spoke very loud, but was not as powerful as the instrument. He therefore called out to the drummer in these words: "Friend, you and I serve the two greatest masters existing, but in different callings; you beat up for volunteers for King George, I for the Lord Jesus. In God's name, then, let us not interrupt each other; the world is wide enough for both, and we may get recruits in abundance." This speech had such an effect on the drummer that he went away in great good humor, and left the preacher in full possession of the field.

[2] The following are the devices and mottoes, as published at the time:

1. A lion erect, a naked cimeter in one paw, the other holding the Pennsylvania scutcheon. Motto: *Patria.*

2. Three arms, wearing different linen, ruffled, plain, and checked, the hands joined by grasping each other's wrist, denoting the union of all ranks. Motto: *Unita Virtus Valet.*

3. An eagle, the emblem of victory, descending from the skies. Motto: *A Deo Victoria.*

4. The figure of Liberty sitting on a cube, holding a spear with the cap of Freedom on its point. Motto: *Inestimabilis.*

5. An armed man with a naked falchion in his hand. Motto: *Deus adjuvat Fortes.*

6. An elephant, being the emblem of a warrior always on his guard, as that creature is said never to lie down and hath his arms ever in readiness. Motto: *Semper Paratus.*

7. A city walled round. Motto: *Solus Patriæ Summa Lex.*

8. A soldier with his piece recovered, ready to present. Motto: *Sic pacem quærimus.*

9. A coronet and plume of feathers. Motto: *In God we trust.*

10. A man with a sword drawn. Motto: *Pro Avis et Focis.*

11. Three of the associators, marching with their muskets shouldered and dressed in different clothes, intimating the unanimity of the different sorts of people in the association. Motto: *Vis Unita Fortior.*

12. A musket and sword crossing each other. Motto: *Pro Rege et Grege.*

13. Representation of a glory, in the middle of which is wrote, JEHOVAH NISSI; in English, *The Lord our Banner.*

14. A castle, at the gate of which a soldier stands sentinel. Motto: *Cavendo Tutus.*

15. David, as he advanced against Goliath and slung the stone. Motto: *In Nomine Domini.*

16. A lion rampant, one paw holding up a cimeter, another a sheaf of wheat. Motto: *Domine Protege Alimentum.*

17. A sleeping lion. Motto: *Rouse me if you dare.*

18. Hope, represented by a woman, standing clothed in blue, holding one hand on an anchor. Motto: *Spero per Deum Vincere.*

19. Duke of Cumberland as a general. Motto: *Pro Deo et Georgia Rege.*

20. A sailor on horseback. Motto: *Pro Libertate Patriæ.*

CHAPTER XI

[1] Dr. Franklin gives a further account of his election in a letter to his son, Governor Franklin, from which the following is an extract:

"LONDON, 19th December, 1767.

"We have had an ugly affair at the Royal Society lately. One Dacosta, a Jew, who, as our clerk, was intrusted with collecting our moneys, had been so unfaithful as to embezzle near thirteen hundred pounds in four years. Being one of the council this year, as well as the last, I have been employed all the last week in attending the inquiry into and unraveling his accounts, in order to come at a full knowledge of his frauds. His securities are bound in one thousand pounds to the society, which they will pay, but we shall probably lose the rest. He had this year received twenty-six admission payments of twenty-five guineas each, which he did not bring to account.

"While attending to this affair I had an opportunity of looking over the old council-books and journals of the society, and having a curiosity to see how I came in, of which I had never been informed, I looked back for the minutes relating to it. You must know it is not usual to admit persons that have not requested to be admitted; and a recommendatory certificate in favor of the candidate, signed by at least three of the members, is by our rule to be presented to the society, expressing that he is desirous of that honor, and is so and so qualified. As I never had asked or expected the honor, I was, as I said before, curious to see how the business was managed. I found that the certificate, worded very advantageously for me, was signed by Lord Macclesfield, then president, Lord Parker, and Lord Willoughby; that the election was by a unanimous vote; and the honor being voluntarily conferred by the society, unsolicited by me, it was thought wrong to demand or receive the usual fees or composition; so that my name was entered on the list with a vote of council *that I was not to pay anything.* And accordingly nothing has ever been demanded of me. Those who are admitted in the common way pay five guineas admission fees and two guineas and a half yearly contributions, or twenty-five guineas down in lieu of it. In my case a substantial favor accompanied the honor." —W. T. F.

CHAPTER XII

[1] In a letter from Dr. Franklin to his wife, dated at Falmouth, the 17th of July, 1757, after giving her a similar account of his voyage, escape, and landing, he adds: "The bell ringing for church we went thither immediately, and with hearts full of gratitude returned sincere thanks to God for the mercies we had received. Were I a Roman Catholic, perhaps I should on this occasion vow to build a chapel to some saint; but as I am not, if I were to vow at all it should be to build a *light-house.*" —W. T. F.

SUGGESTED READING

ANDERSON, DOUGLAS. *The Radical Enlightenments of Benjamin Franklin.* Baltimore, MD: Johns Hopkins University Press, 1997.

BRANDS, H. W. *The First American: The Life and Times of Benjamin Franklin.* New York: Doubleday, 2000.

CLARK, RONALD. *Benjamin Franklin.* New York: Barnes & Noble Books, 2004.

ISAACSON, WALTER. *Benjamin Franklin: An American Life.* New York: Simon & Schuster, 2003.

MIDDLEKAUFF, ROBERT. *Benjamin Franklin and His Enemies.* Berkeley, CA: University of California Press, 1996.

SEAVEY, ORMOND. *Becoming Benjamin Franklin: The Autobiography and the Life.* University Park, PA: Pennsylvania State University Press, 1988.

SPENGEMANN, WILLIAM C. *The Forms of Autobiography.* New Haven, CT: Yale University Press, 1980.

WALTERS, KERRY S. *Benjamin Franklin and His Gods.* Urbana, IL: University of Illinois Press, 1999.

WOOD, GORDON. *The Americanization of Benjamin Franklin.* New York: Penguin Press, 2004.